CHICAGOISMS
THE CITY AS CATALYST FOR ARCHITECTURAL SPECULATION

DESIGN AND TYPOGRAPHY: Jörg Becker, Chicago
EDITOR: Ria Stein, Berlin
TYPEFACE: DINOT Condensed; Utopia Std Caption; Utopia Old Style Figures
LITHOGRAPHY, PRINTING, AND BINDING: DZA Druckerei zu Altenburg GmbH, Thüringen

Park Books
Niederdorfstrasse 54
CH-8001 Zürich
Switzerland
www.park-books.com

ISBN 978-3-906027-15-9

ALEXANDER EISENSCHMIDT
WITH JONATHAN MEKINDA (EDS.)

CHICAGOISMS
THE CITY AS CATALYST FOR ARCHITECTURAL SPECULATION

 PARK BOOKS

PREFACE

STANLEY TIGERMAN

The ambition of this book is to position Chicago within a critical global framework beyond (but not excluding) the structures that are built by the city's architects. In order to accomplish that goal, internationally respected historians, critics, and theorists are placed squarely into the flame of Chicago's renowned architectural cauldron to weigh in on "the anxiety of influence," both coming in to and going out from Chicago and the hothouse incubator that is this city.

  Within the history of architecture, Chicago has been typically positioned as the fertile ground out of which the flame of modernism burst after the majority of the central city burned down in 1871. In this story, "ambulance chasers" from the East Coast such as Louis Sullivan and P. B. Wight converged on the ruins, offering their services to assist in transforming our cow town. Because the need to rebuild swiftly was so pressing, architectural flourishes and ornamental embellishments were either frowned upon or considered unnecessary. While that urgent need flew in the face of Chicagoans' insecurities about their self-conscious lack of enculturation, pragmatism prevailed and Chicago was rebuilt expediently. The coincidence of cast iron and electric elevators buttressed a new method of constructing tall buildings and with the help of William Le Baron Jenney, Holabird and Roche, and others–Presto!–the (first) "Chicago School" of architecture and modernism more generally was hatched, or so claimed a much-later generation of architectural historians.

  Half a century later (and challenging attempts to gentrify the city by such events as the Columbian Exhibition and "The City Beautiful" movement), architectural historians (led by Carl Condit) presented Chicago's architects as single-mindedly structurally driven and constructionally motivated. Chicago's reputation was fixed in a no-nonsense, practical, "modernist" way of making buildings. During the Great Depression, and five years after his being lauded at New York's Museum of Modern Art's 1932 "International Style" exhibition, Ludwig Mies van der Rohe arrived (together with Ludwig Hilberseimer and Walter Peterhans) to direct the architecture school at Armour Institute (later the Illinois Institute of Technology [IIT]).

  Subsequently, Chicago's place in the firmament was solidified by the production of buildings and (not insignificantly) students who would constitute the second "Chicago School" of architecture. The result was that the city's architectural reputation was rigidly codified through the first three quarters of the twentieth century. And just like that, Chicago was transmuted from a cow town to a Mies metropolis.

Inevitably, there were mumblings and grumblings about any "one *right* way to build." Chicago architects reacted against this rigid version of history and began to understand again that they were a part of a nexus larger than any one city and a single, self-imposed, pragmatic label could possibly represent. With the 1966 publication of Robert Venturi's game-changing book *Complexity and Contradiction in Architecture*, which was followed three years later by Mies van der Rohe's death, the stranglehold that Mies's acolytes held on the city began to come apart. This was particularly true with respect to a new breed of influential academics whose strength was architectural theory and criticism – not simply building – and who challenged the suffocating narrative of the "Chicago Schools."

Toward the end of the twentieth century and the beginning of the twenty-first, a new generation of studio critics not trained as architects came to prominence. Beatriz Colomina, Joan Copjec, Catherine Ingraham, Sarah Herda, Jeffrey Kipnis, Sanford Kwinter, Sylvia Lavin, Joan Ockman, Zoë Ryan, Robert Somol, Michael Speaks, John Whiteman, and others helped to bring criticism and theory into a seminal position within the design studios of the architectural academy and push beyond the orthodox history of the city. Ingraham and Somol taught at the University of Illinois at Chicago (UIC) in the 1980s and early 1990s, with Somol now the Director of Architecture at UIC, and lo-and-behold (!), Chicago's reputation morphed into that of a city that now welcomed differentiated points of view, from both a theoretical and an actualized point of view. This book, with its collection of essays that take us across the globe will do much to enhance this newly recognized aspect of the character of the city; since character looms large in the way in which perceptions are formed as they focus their gaze once again on Chicago.

PALACE OF CULTURE

ROBERT BRUEGMANN

If I had to pick a single building that best exemplifies Chicago's contribution to modern architecture and world history, I would argue for the Auditorium Building. Erected less than sixty years after the city's founding, the Auditorium was a palace of culture that overshadowed New York's Metropolitan Opera House and rivaled anything to be seen in the European capitals. It marked a triumphant conclusion to the city's era of greatest economic and population growth and the moment when the city determined to compete in the world of culture. Although it emerged during a period of social turbulence and vast income inequality, its patrons imagined it as a place where all strata of society could comfortably mingle. They achieved this goal in part through a highly unusual design in which the theater was subsidized by an office structure and hotel that wrapped around it on three sides. Looming above the lakefront, it was the largest building in Chicago and, with its 240-foot tower, the tallest. With its structural ingenuity, for example the way the Banquet Hall was suspended over the auditorium, its innovative mechanical and stage equipment, and its acoustic refinements, all the work of Dankmar Adler, it incorporated some of the most advanced technological thinking of the day. Above all, it was an aesthetic triumph. Within its hard masonry shell of relatively reserved Richardsonian Romanesque arches, lay the splendid, almost barbarically rich decoration Louis Sullivan devised for the principal spaces of the theater and the hotel. Of the auditorium itself, Frank Lloyd Wright, who worked in the Adler & Sullivan office during its creation, opined that it was the "greatest room for music and opera in the world." For once in his life Wright could not be accused of overstatement. With its accumulation of gilt surfaces, frescoes, stenciled decoration, and concentric arcs of golden light bulbs, it must have presented an overwhelming sensation on the day of its inaugural. It still does.

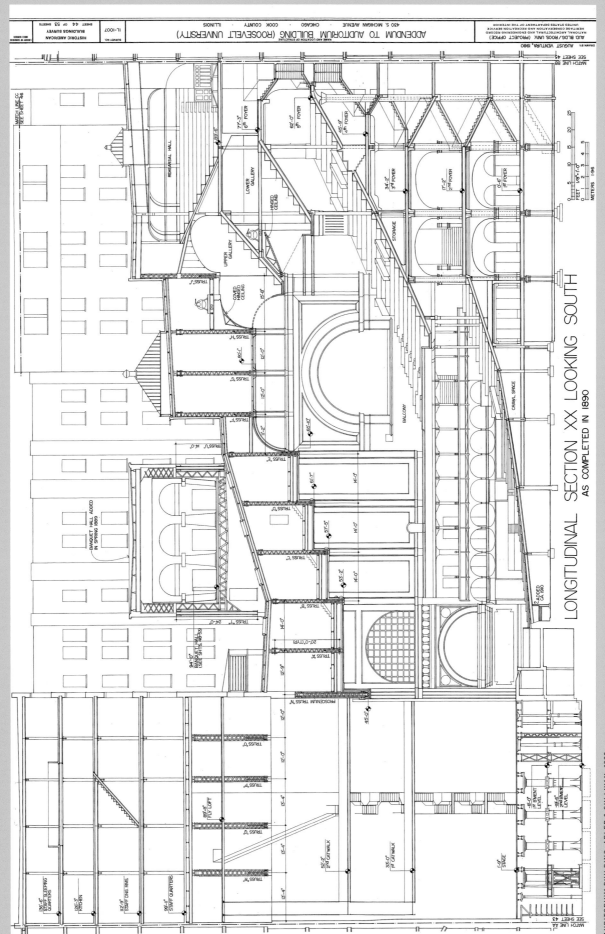

LONGITUDINAL SECTION XX LOOKING SOUTH
AS COMPLETED IN 1890

AUDITORIUM BUILDING, ADLER & SULLIVAN, 1889.

SELF-EQUILIBRATING SPECTACLE

WILLIAM F. BAKER

When Daniel H. Burnham first met George W. G. Ferris, he was nearly drowning in the expense and enormity of his plans for the World's Columbian Exposition of 1893. Burnham had challenged American engineers to create a monument that would do for Chicago what French engineer Gustave Eiffel had done for Paris at the Exposition Universelle of 1889. He needed something unique and profitable, and he needed it quick. Ferris's response? A revolving passenger wheel, 250 feet in diameter, that would reach taller than any of Chicago's buildings and carry over two thousand people at a time. This "Ferris" Wheel, as much an idea as a structure, was an immediate success and had a profound cultural and commercial impact: while there is only one Eiffel Tower, there are many Ferris Wheels today. Completed on time and within budget, it exemplifies in extreme clarity the condition of a self-equilibrating structure in which the very elements that hold the structure together at the same time threaten to tear it apart.

Ferris had not only a daring idea, but also the ambition and the knowledge to execute it. His unique combination of passion and pragmatism is emblematic of Chicago, and his wheel is an ideal metaphor for the city. Here in Chicago the confluence of knowledge and ambition, of daring spirit and pragmatism generates a kind of self-equilibrating urban structure in which the forces for growth and change that strain the fabric of the city are the selfsame forces that hold it together and push it into the future.

INTRODUCTION: CHICAGO AS IDEA

ALEXANDER EISENSCHMIDT AND JONATHAN MEKINDA

Throughout its relatively short urban history, Chicago has mesmerized people around the world as both a symbol and embodiment of the modern metropolis. This collection of essays takes exactly this power of the city as its subject and explores the influence and impact of the idea of Chicago. Long celebrated as the birthplace of modern architecture in America, Chicago is the subject of a remarkable body of work, both scholarly and popular, exploring the history of architecture and urbanism in the city. Ranging from monographs on the city's most important inhabitants and events to more methodologically varied explorations of specific building types, local architectural "schools," and the impact of various social, economic, and natural forces on the growth of the city, most of these works focus on factors internal to the city and its local and regional context. This focus, in turn, reinforces the popular notion that Chicago is a particularly and uniquely American, even Midwestern, urban formation, a notion that is not only fundamental to the reputation of the city, but also central to the stories that Chicago tells about itself. This conception of the city, however, largely fails to account both for the diverse ways in which outsiders have engaged Chicago and for the tremendous impact that the city has had in other contexts – national and international. Indeed, it appears that the well-rehearsed and widely repeated narrative of Chicago's architectural development often prevents understanding the city in relationship to other forces.

Rather than celebrating the city's rootedness in a distinct regional environment, this collection of essays interrogates Chicago's connectedness to a larger global network of people and institutions, forces and ideas. In particular, it focuses on two aspects of the life of the city that are often overlooked, namely its remarkable power as a transmitter of ideas about the modern city and its particular capacity to foment radical architectural and urban visions. Having served as a source of inspiration and a site of activity for architects, urbanists, and theorists around the globe, Chicago is here examined for its ability to act constructively as a mediator of ideas – an architectural broadcaster of sorts – and as an instigator of speculation – a kind of urban incubator.

Chicago's engagement with the world performs then in two directions: away from the city, via its activity as an exporter of architectural and urban ideas, and toward it, by offering the city as a test-bed for speculative agendas imported from abroad. Adolf Loos and Frank Lloyd Wright are just two of the many figures who demonstrate how the city operates in these capacities. Loos visited the city in 1893 to see the World's Columbian Exposition using money his mother only gave him on the condition that he never return home, while Wright abandoned his established life and practice in the city when he left for Europe in 1909. Both acted as carriers of ideas: Loos absorbed the lessons of the so-called "Chicago School" and brought the ideas of Sullivan to Europe, while Wright's Wasmuth Portfolio linked international modernism forever to the American Midwest. Eventually, Loos and Wright also returned to Chicago with more radical proposals for the Tribune Tower of 1922 and the National Life Insurance Building in 1924 respectively. For both architects, Chicago not only provided a critical impulse for their excursions–acting as an accelerator to the transmission of their architectural agendas–but also offered solid ground for the projection of their speculative proposals.

Recounting Loos's and Wright's relationship with the city offers a preliminary glimpse of Chicago's power as a springboard for urban and architectural dreams that was rooted in its commitment to commercial progress, openness to technological experimentation, and willingness to reinvent itself – qualities manifested in such projects as the raising of the city's ground plane in the 1860s, the reversing of the Chicago River in the 1890s, and the almost constant expansion of the city on landfill during the 1910s and 1920s. It was precisely these kinds of projects that, along with its unprecedented pace of growth (from a frontier village to the sixth-largest city in the world in only seven decades), made Chicago one of the most widely celebrated and most frequently visited examples of the industrial metropolis. Some visitors remained in the city permanently, most just stayed briefly, and others only "visited" with the help of media such as postcards, photographs, and movies. All of them, however, were eager to find in Chicago the future that still lay ahead for most cities.

Indeed, the imaginative capacity of the city is such that Chicago has inspired projects elsewhere that were not even considered possible at home. Hans Hollein, for example, spent much of the year he lived in Chicago during the late 1950s re-imagining the famous tall buildings of the city, first embracing and then re-deploying the conventions of the type. His "Skyscraper of the Future" project from that year split the conventional tower into segments to accommodate gardens and public spaces and other programs in the air. After more than fifty years in Hollein's sketchbook–preserved and ready for resuscitation–the scheme is currently under construction in Shenzhen, China. This is just one instance of the actualization of Loos's assertion about his own Tribune Tower proposal: "It must be built! If not in Chicago, then in some other town."

Chicagoisms, the title of this volume, refers precisely to those moments of productive interaction and wild provocation, of radical speculation and fruitful exchange, that Chicago is uniquely capable of inspiring and fostering–a power well demonstrated by the sheer number of proposals that take the city as a launch-pad for urban and architectural imaginings. In the "Chicagoisms" considered here, selective episodes in the history of the city are interrogated with the explicit aim of shedding light on the internal workings, dynamics, and forces that have made Chicago such a site of possibility. To that end, this volume brings together two types of studies: on the one hand essays that explore particular figures, ideas, and events, and on the other hand shorter, more speculative commentaries on a number of the city's best-known projects.

13

The distinction between these two components is not simply a matter of scale, but also of orientation: while most of the essays look at the city from the outside-in, the commentaries inserted between them proceed from the inside-out to address the works' broader influences and capacities. Drawing on both new research and new readings of already familiar projects, this collection aims to break open the conventional and hermetic narrative of Chicago's architecture and urbanism to reveal a condition that resonates in different cities, fields, and practices.

The opening essays by Penelope Dean and Igor Marjanović revisit events of the 1960s and 1970s that profoundly influenced the architectural discourse of the late twentieth century. For Dean, two exhibitions presented concurrently in 1976 demonstrate the stagnation of the established history of Chicago's architecture and, simultaneously, enable her to unearth alternative legacies within that history. Marjanović focuses on events of a different nature in his examination of Alvin Boyarsky's tenure at the University of Illinois at Chicago during the tumultuous years of the late 1960s. He shows how Boyarsky's embrace of the vitality and dynamism of the city, rather than its architectural traditions, inspired his subsequent activity as the Director of the Architectural Association in London, where he revolutionized the organization of the school and, ultimately, shaped contemporary avant-garde practices through his work with figures such as Zaha Hadid, Rem Koolhaas, and Bernard Tschumi.

If the essays by Dean and Marjanović highlight Chicago's capacity to shape architectural discourse and reorganize conceptions of the city, the essays by John Harwood, Mark Linder, and Albert Pope all take up specific design projects. Pope's study of Chicago-based projects by Ludwig Hilberseimer reveals a fostered proximity between urban forms that are commonly in opposition. The modern city visions that Hilberseimer drew up in Germany before arriving in the US found in Chicago a new foil that consolidated previously opposing urban environments (the dense center vs. the distributed suburb). What Pope describes here is a kind of super-urbanism, highly productive for contemporary practice in our time of extreme urbanization. Mark Linder's text moves from the Chicago of Hilberseimer and Mies van der Rohe to the England of Reyner Banham and Allison and Peter Smithson, uncovering the intersecting lines between New Brutalism and the Chicago modernism of Mies. Ultimately, Linder constructs a new genealogy that rethinks both movements and exposes unknown, even exotic, tendencies within each. Another colleague of Mies and Hilberseimer at the Illinois Institute of Technology is at the center of John Harwood's essay, which focuses on Konrad Wachsmann's ventures into early digital experiments and its possible effects on architecture. Harwood suggests that these proto-computational models were the first attempts to calibrate architecture around research principles and cybernetics, practices that would only gain substantial currency much later.

In the final set of essays, Joanna Merwood-Salisbury, David Haney, and Alexander Eisenschmidt consider earlier aspects of Chicago's architecture and urbanism, particularly in relationship to the city's reception elsewhere. Merwood-Salisbury's analysis of the *Early Modern Architecture: Chicago 1870–1910* exhibition at the Museum of Modern Art in New York in 1933 explores what she describes as a process of "naturalization" through which the modern architecture of Europe was stripped of any association with radical politics and rooted instead in American capitalism. With this transformation, Chicago became a key accomplice in the creation of the myth of the "International Style." Like the "Chicago School," celebrated by Hitchcock and Johnson, Daniel Burnham's *Plan of Chicago* (1909) is another of the city's "urban legends." Focusing on the travels of the plan across Europe in the wake of its publication, Haney examines its reception in London, Paris, and Berlin, where it functioned as an industrious piece of architectural propaganda. As this essay shows, it was impossible to talk about the state of the city at the turn of the twentieth century without referring to Chicago. But even before Burnham's *Plan*, Chicago had become for many cities abroad the measure of urban modernity. The final essay considers how the city became the model through which Berlin was able to understand its own rapid urbanization during the late nineteenth century and, ultimately, reconceive itself as a space of possibilities for the invention of a metropolitan architecture.

The essays gathered here stray from the well-trodden paths of Chicago's history to explore lesser known episodes and a wider range of actors and artifacts, from architects to exhibitions, from books to punch cards. The objective here is not to give yet another summation of Chicago's history, but to open up a new discussion about the potentials generated by the city itself. In order to amplify the multiplicity of readings afforded by Chicago and its various "isms," short pieces of writing that comment on specific projects are inserted between the essays. Forming a quasi-independent catalogue of projects, the commentaries articulate an alternative structure, parallel to the essays, that aims to resituate a number of Chicago's already well-known works within the particular framework of this collection.

The commentaries begin with Robert Bruegmann, who finds sensation in Adler & Sullivan's Auditorium Building, and continue as William Baker locates equilibrium in the world's first "Ferris Wheel." Sandy Isenstadt measures the achievement of the Chicago Sanitary and Ship Canal, Winy Maas detects an accelerated grid in Burnham's *Plan of Chicago*, and Brett Steele celebrates Frank Lloyd Wright's Wasmuth Folio as the first modern architectural monograph. The catalogue of projects continues with Sam Jacob's interrogation of Loos's Tribune Tower and Bart Lootsma's discovery of the Dymaxion House by Buckminster Fuller at Marshall Field's Department Store, and then turns to several iconic mid-century projects as Barry Bergdoll investigates the skeletal frame of Mies's Lake Shore Drive Apartments, Alexander Eisenschmidt contemplates the urbanism of the Circle Interchange, and David Lewis glimpses metropolitan suburbia at Marina City by Bertrand Goldberg. At mid-point in the book, Kazys Varnelis enters the airborne city of SOM's Hancock Tower and Aaron Betsky raises Tigerman's *Titanic* once more.

The remainder of the catalogue looks at projects offered to the city more recently: Mirko Zardini explores Greg Lynn's final pre-digital experiment for the Stranded Sears Tower project, Sarah Whiting roams the spatial graphics of ITT's McCormick Campus Center by OMA, Ellen Grimes defines a "Chicago Style" via Doug Garofalo's Hyde Park Art Center, Sylvia Lavin suggests we cannot avoid paying attention to Anish Kapoor's Cloud Gate, Mark Lee interprets UN Studio's Burnham Centennial Pavilion in Millenium Park as a new kind of "primitive hut," and Andres Lepik finds a new type of skyscraper in Studio Gang's Aqua Tower. The final two commentaries consider even more recent proposals for Chicago: UrbanLAB's "Free Water District" and "Environmental Typologies" by Weathers. In the former, John McMorrough sees an abundance of possibilities in a world of limits, while the latter gives Pedro Gadanho reason to hope for a renewed attention to the tangible effects of atmosphere. Covering only a small selection of the register of important works in Chicago, the catalogue of projects nonetheless presents a case for the city's power as an instigator of ideas and generator of opportunities for speculation. As this register of projects proceeds from the nineteenth century toward the present, it also aims to act as a call for future proposals.

Together, the essays and commentaries gathered in this collection probe the extent of Chicago's capacity to spark the imaginations of architects and engineers, artists and urbanists, and to foster the spread and cross-fertilization of ideas about the modern city. This approach to the city as an idea–as an intellectual concept as much as a physical phenomenon–does not overturn the established history of Chicago so much as it supplements and complicates that history. As the various episodes and projects considered here show, the idea of Chicago was both powerful and adaptable, serving as a harbinger of architectural and urban worlds to come and spurring a range of actions and activities beyond the city as well as within it. In the light of these "Chicagoisms," the city no longer stands as only an American formation, but must be seen within an international discourse about the industrial and later post-industrial city and the architecture appropriate for it. By virtue of its status as an iconic modern metropolis, with all of the horrors and dreams associated with that urban configuration, Chicago profoundly shaped–and was shaped by–that discourse.

The tension between the "positive" and "negative" aspects of modernity that Chicago has so clearly displayed to the world since the early nineteenth century is paralleled by another tension no less fundamental to the way that the city has developed: that between the demand for action and the desire for refinement. Many of the city's most famous projects resulted from efforts to engage problems of the modern world through the most efficient and straightforward means possible, often resulting in radical formations of urbanism and architecture. Others, in contrast, were motivated by the desire to repair, if not counteract, exactly that pragmatic impulse and its "ugly" consequences. From the vantage point of today, however, it seems clear that Chicago's maturing has brought an increased caution toward its previous restless-ness and ambition to extrapolate modern conditions. Taking this observation seriously, this collection not only aims to trace the characteristics, attitudes, and mentalities that made Chicago and captivated other cities, but also hopes to channel a renewed boldness to engage the city's history as well as today's urbanized world in general. To counter the increased caution of the city, perhaps what is needed is a move from "Chicagoisms" to "Chicagoism," that is the extraction from the episodes considered here of a more abstract but widely applicable theorem or principle of action that recognizes and engages the city as a catalyst. "Chicagoism," then, would emphasize the operative function of the city as a construct that is effective beyond the city's own bounds, providing the ground for experimentation and releasing ideas into the urban and architectural ether.

UPSTREAM

SANDY ISENSTADT

18

Beginning in 1900, Chicago's moral sensibility began to drain westward from the city at a maximum rate of ten thousand cubic feet per second. At least, Victor Hugo might have seen it that way, based on his view of the sewers of Paris as the conscience of the city, where everything converges and confronts everything else in its most definitive form. Chicago had neither the benefit of centuries to develop its system for managing human waste nor did it have an agreeable geology. The need for a large-scale solution to the city's waste problem had long been apparent. But not until engineers were emboldened, one imagines, by towers touching the sky, would they begin in earnest to permanently reverse the course of the Chicago River. The result was a network of waterways, the Sanitary and Ship Canal, an achievement that stands as one of the greatest public works projects since Rome threaded Southern Europe with a network of aqueducts. It was also a contentious project, spawning lawsuits from upstream, by Great Lakes states concerned about lowered water levels, and downstream, by cities destined to receive Chicago's effluvium. As a result, the project led courts to begin to ponder questions of environmental significance. And it remains so, as the various invasive species of Asian carp follow the Canal to threaten the ecology of the Great Lakes. But that was all to come. At the start of the twentieth century the Canal, an unhidden container of flowing wastewater, allowed Chicago to continue its remarkable boom without the burden of compunction.

CHICAGO SANITARY AND SHIP CANAL, ISHAM RANDOLPH AND THE SANITARY DISTRICT OF CHICAGO, 1900.

ACCELERATED GRID

WINY MAAS

20

By the end of the nineteenth century, the majority of European capitals had undergone one of the most dramatic spurts of urbanization in history. To better understand this development, many Europeans studied the American metropolis as a trendsetter, just as the historic European city had been a source for earlier American proposals. With Burnham's *Plan of Chicago*, the direction of influence reversed once again, producing a "collaged" urbanism that combined the wisdom of Ildefons Cerdà's Barcelona with that of André Le Nôtre's pre- and Georges-Eugène Haussmann's post-revolutionary Paris.

The plan, however, does not only hint at an amusing eclecticism that is heavily compromised by a wish for a misplaced symmetry (one may ask what this axis is pointing to at the other side of the lake?) and the urge for a Civic Center (at the location of today's Circle Interchange, one of the most trafficked intersections). It also suggests the possibility of accelerating the grid through occasional densification and sweeping diagonal connections that zigzag across the city. While sometimes compromising the logics of the rectilinear system, these elements suggest the potential of a mini-grid that allows for more public surface and hyper-access. Is this suggesting the first network city? The result is a new kind of urban porosity that offsets common density by activating smaller entities to reign freely within the block.

PLAN OF CHICAGO, DANIEL H. BURNHAM AND EDWARD H. BENNETT, 1909.

THAT '70S SHOW

PENELOPE DEAN

On consecutive days in spring 1976, two exhibitions opened in Chicago that would propose opposed legacies for the city's architectural history, and potentially for its future lines of development. *100 Years of Architecture in Chicago: Continuity of Structure and Form*, organized by Skidmore, Owings & Merrill (SOM) architect Peter Pran and Chicago critic Franz Schulze, opened at the Museum of Contemporary Art (MCA) on May 1 as an expanded American version of Oswald W. Grube's 1973 Munich exhibition of the same name. Presenting a chronological history of Chicago architecture, it began with the engineering considerations of the first "Chicago School," passed through the legacy of Mies van der Rohe (the second "Chicago School"), and culminated in the corporate architectural generation following Mies, of which the offices of SOM and C. F. Murphy Associates were emblematic. In a sequential approach to the lineage of steel-frame construction, the exhibition ordered architectural history through the methodology of historicism, producing a linear narrative of origins. The second exhibition, simply titled *Chicago Architects*, was organized by a group of local practitioners – Stanley Tigerman, Stuart Cohen, Larry Booth, and Ben Weese – and opened in the lobby of Harry Weese's Time-Life Building on April 30.[1] Conceived polemically as a counter-exhibition to *100 Years*, it showcased a selection of buildings, chosen primarily for idea and aesthetic merit, formal rather than just technological significance.[2] Declaring the city's architectural history to be wider and more inclusive than the persistence of "structure and form," Tigerman and Cohen curated a miscellany of projects under different terms in a non-linear arrangement. Despite the work of some architects appearing in both *100 Years* and *Chicago Architects* (e.g. Bertrand Goldberg and Harry Weese), significantly the latter show did not claim a singular origin point or teleology but reassembled historic sources through the technique of genealogy rather than historicism.[3]

The two exhibitions demonstrate that architectural history can both repress and enable ideas in a public context. As Tigerman asks in his introductory catalogue essay *"Salon des Refusés"* (1976), has Chicago architecture consciously been removed from the mainstream of architecture by tastemakers protective of their own role in the modern movement? Has obscure, seminal work been exorcized from the liturgy so as to canonize well-known celebrants?[4] Arguing that Chicago's architectural history had excluded alternative work outside the "sweeping use of the skeleton frame," Tigerman countered that while other, equally significant architectural ideas had stemmed from Chicago (e.g. pre-Venturi shingle style architecture and post-Prairie school vernacular), such ideas were largely ignored by historians (e.g. Colin Rowe and Carl Condit) for not fitting into a lineage of steel-frame construction.[5] Peter Pran's *100 Years*

catalogue essay, "Introduction to the American Exhibition," exemplified this assessment: "Chicago's most significant contribution to modern architecture has been a rational approach to form and space [...] which stresses the derivation of the look of the building from the structural elements that compose it."[6] In response to this restrictive canon, the aims of the *Chicago Architects* show, as Cohen remarked more recently, "were to rewrite history and to undermine a position of power that existed for Murphy and SOM and IIT."[7] In this regard, the counter-show not only attempted to retell the history of Chicago architecture and "how the history had been written by Giedion and

Pevsner and later by Oswald Grube to be one thing to the exclusion of another thing,"[8] but also articulated a perceived power imbalance between two groups of practicing architects, that is between a domineering corporate office culture promoted by Pran, Schulze, and Grube as Mies's legacy, and a smaller, alternative culture launched by Tigerman and company in search of more eclectic roots. For Tigerman and Cohen in particular, the relentless promotion of a singular version of Chicago's architectural history had fueled this professional disparity.

As teleological history was perceived to repress the possibilities for a younger generation of practitioners, the revisionist history put forward by Tigerman, Cohen, and others was inversely conceived as a prospective activity: an attempt to create the space for alternative forms of contemporary practice. As historian Craig Owens suggested in another context, the goal of any Nietzschean genealogy, like modernism itself, was not "to re-animate or restore the past; rather, [... it] was fundamentally a clearing operation, [...] an attempt to clear a space in which the new might emerge."[9]

COVER OF *CHICAGO ARCHITECTS*, EXHIBITION CATALOGUE, 1976.

And so for the *Chicago Architects* curators, the deployment of architectural history was less about re-asserting an architectural past than it was an act of design, one that might open up the possibility for another architectural future. In opposition to the "myopic" construction of history, as Stuart Cohen characterized it,[10] and as a corrective to the oversimplification and misrepresentation of history as Tigerman put it,[11] *Chicago Architects* represents an attempt to design an alternate prospect for practice, an ideas-driven disciplinary project rather than one steered by the normative environment of the professional building industry. For it was the corporate generation of Mies's followers that Tigerman and Cohen were at odds with (not Mies himself) for reducing architecture (and Mies's conceptual project) to the pragmatic concerns of construction. This attempt to re-orient the discipline back to the world of ideas quickly mobilized into a broader platform for design innovation with the formation by Tigerman and his cohort into the "Chicago Seven" by December 1976.[12] It was succinctly portrayed in Tigerman's graphic polemic the *Titanic* (1978), a photomontage depicting the sinking of Mies's Crown Hall into Lake Michigan. And it represents a productive moment when ideas were paramount, where specific versions of architectural history intersected with professional practice, and where the styling of history enabled architectural ideas to reach a broader public.

  Rather than justify the continuity of a particular tradition, this rewriting of Chicago's architectural history as something other than a lineage of steel-frame construction formed part of an ambition to ignite a culture of architectural debate in

100 Years of Architecture in Chicago
Continuity of Structure and Form

by Oswald W. Grube, Peter C. Pran and Franz Schulze

COVER OF *100 YEARS OF ARCHITECTURE: CONTINUITY OF STRUCTURE AND FORM*, EXHIBITION CATALOGUE, 1976.

Chicago at the very moment when, as Tigerman put it, "the varieties and kinds of interchange that, among other things, produce a richness that might just spark a new movement, meet a silent 'still-birth'";[13] or as Cohen later characterized the Chicago scene, a "kind of black, Miesian silence."[14] In this sense *Chicago Architects* was an attempt to agitate and infuse a local architectural discourse with energy, and to end a "build, don't talk" reception of Mies's message. For Tigerman, there was a particular necessity to re-claim the intellectual content of Chicago's modern architecture from what he perceived as "a proprietary treatment of architectural history by east coast intellectuals" who had "disposed of Chicago Architecture by tossing it the bone of the skeleton frame, while keeping for themselves the 'idea content' of the modern movement."[15] The construction and subsequent reception of a re-directed architectural history would ostensibly put the Chicago architecture scene finally on the national map on *its* own terms.

The staging of the two exhibitions, with their concurrent openings and conflicting versions of history, provided the foundation for an elevated local discourse, one that would inevitably reach a broader audience, as evidenced by record exhibition attendance and the number and range of reviews covering the exhibitions between February 1975 and December 1976. The architectural culture produced by and around the exhibitions themselves–the catalogues, reviews, and press coverage–appeared as architectural production and discourse began to expand beyond the boundaries of academic design established by modernism. Following on the heels of the Whites

26   STANLEY TIGERMAN, *THE TITANIC*, 1978.

versus Grays architectural debates that had taken place in New York in 1974, in which the Whites had advocated for a modernist legacy of formal purity, while the Grays promoted a post-modernist trajectory of eclecticism,[16] the Chicago exhibitions and their catalogues, openings, and press coverage framed a much more accessible debate. Crossing publication genres and constituencies–academic, professional, popular–the exhibition face-off provides lessons for the production and dissemination of architectural culture beyond the academy today.

FORMAT

While the catalogues for both *100 Years* and *Chicago Architects* cover the same century of architectural development in Chicago, they deploy different yet oddly complementary formatting strategies. The *Chicago Architects* catalogue, designed by John Massey, has the same proportions as the *100 Years* catalogue, though it is slightly larger. Its wrap-around cover featuring a grid of tightly cropped photographs of architect's faces replicates the similarly gridded biographic back matter of the *100 Years* catalogue, which features sixty participants' faces (indeed, some of the photographs are identical). Yet by bringing portraits of forty-seven architects to the front of the catalogue, *Chicago Architects* pointedly shifts Chicago's architectural history away from a narrative of "structure and form" (as represented by the building detail on the *100 Years* cover), toward one centered on individual personalities. Indeed, as the title "Chicago Architects" and mosaic of portraits on the cover of the catalogue suggest, the eclectic

27 VIEWS OF THE THOMAS H. GALA HOUSE BY FRANK LLOYD WRIGHT (LEFT) AND THE FIRST BAPTIST CHURCH BY HARRY WEESE (RIGHT) IN *CHICAGO ARCHITECTS*, 1976. THIS SPREAD ILLUSTRATES THE FORMAL SIMILARITIES BETWEEN THE ROOFS OF THE TWO BUILDINGS.

historical content of the exhibition is held together in part through a notion of authorship. In this sense the catalogue's cover portraits reveal the more plastic technique of genealogy and help account for the eclectic selection of small structures (houses, schools, and churches) included in the exhibition. Internally, the authored projects collectively emphasize formal and stylistic elements over strict chronology and are sequenced in compare-contrast layouts where, for example, the extruded brick-bays of Barry Nyrne appear opposite those of Ben Weese, the soft corners of Andrew Rebori sit next to those of George Fred Keck and William Keck, and pitched roofs by Frank Lloyd Wright are adjacent to those of Harry Weese. In an effort to communicate spatial and symbolic associations beyond structure and form to a broader public, the represented projects appear in large black-and-white photographs, and occasional line drawings set without lengthy textual explanations.[17] By foregrounding authorship and stylistic elements over structure and form, the *Chicago Architects* catalogue assembles a heterogeneous architectural history.

The *100 Years* catalogue is a denser and more book-like volume containing an interwoven distribution of essays, captions, and images. In contrast to the portraits of *Chicago Architects*, a silver and black, zoomed-in photograph on the cover depicts a gridded curtain-wall and affirms that "structure and form" is unmistakably the exhibition's organizing theme. Internally, projects proceed by strict chronology through the two "Chicago Schools," largely consisting of corporate examples of steel-frame

**860–880 Lake Shore Drive Apartments
1948–51
Mies van der Rohe
(with Pace Assoc. and Holsman,
Klekamp & Taylor)**

None of Mies van der Rohe's buildings had as immediate or as powerful an impact on his American contemporaries as his two 26-story apartment towers at 860–880 Lake Shore Drive. In the consistency and simplicity of their expression Mies proved that his vision in the 1920s—of an architecture based on a distillate of structure—was not a Utopian impossibility but a bold prediction of the future. Thus the significance of these buildings lies not so much in the sophistication of their technology and structure as in the compelling formal—one might say abstract—*expression* of structure and technology.

Walther Peterhans, who taught with Mies at I.I.T., said, "These towers testify to a new and until now unknown spirit. They are built out of the familiar materials, steel and glass, and yet it is as though they introduce the era of steel and glass, as if steel and glass are seen for the first time."

The steel structural elements of the towers are sheathed with concrete fireproofing. Load-bearing irretrievable formwork of galvanized steel clads the concrete, and helps reduce the sway factor present in tall structures. Thus the black-painted steel skin, welded without horizontal joints, is a direct expression of concealed structural function. Prefabricated in sections one column bay wide and two stories high, the facade elements were hoisted up at the site, and welded to the skeleton, making possible the absorption throughout its entire mass of interior and exterior temperature differentials. Finally, aluminum framed windows were fitted to

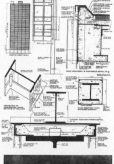

the steel mullions. Off-white, light-reflecting curtains intensify the contrast between skeleton and glazing.

The wide column spacing permits

flexible and open apartment plans in these buildings; all utilities and mechanical spaces are concentrated within the interior bays. Large windows, extending from floor to ceiling, bring the resident into direct visual contact with his environment, the most dramatic element of which is the great sweep of Lake Michigan.

Almost without exception in his later tall buildings, Mies abandoned the type of facade of which 860–880 was the prototype in favor of equally-spaced aluminum curtain walls which conceal the dimensions and placement of the structural frame. Although he chose

this direction first revealed in the alternate proposal for the Promontory Apartments, the lesson of 860–880 in continuing the structural expression found in the great buildings of the first Chicago school was grasped and carried forth by a succeeding generation —most notably by Mies's pupil Jacques Brownson.

**Inland Steel Building 1957
30 W. Monroe
Skidmore, Owings & Merrill
(Bruce Graham, designer in charge)**

The curtain wall as a uniform and unarticulated envelope for skeleton structures has found less acceptance in Chicago than in other large American and European cities. While such facades may be a logical consequence of economical prefabrication techniques, architectural developments in Chicago in the last decade have proved that the clear architectonic expression of structure often results in facades which are also structurally superior. In the Inland Steel Building, the first architecturally significant high rise in the Loop since the days of the first Chicago school, the building's form and architectonic expression reflect not only its structure but a completely new solution to internal function. The 10,000 sq. ft. (930 m²) area of the 17 floors is completely column-free and can be subdivided with prefabricated moveable partitions. All load-bearing supports are positioned outside the facade, and all mechanical and service rooms, stairs and elevators are concentrated in an asymmetrically-placed 25-story service tower. Over a third of the site remains open at the ground floor as an extension of the pedestrian area.

SPREAD FROM *100 YEARS OF ARCHITECTURE: CONTINUITY OF STRUCTURE AND FORM*, 1976. THIS SPREAD ILLUSTRATES THE CONTINUITY OF STEEL-FRAME CONSTRUCTION IN CHICAGO FROM MIES VAN DER ROHE'S 860-880 LAKE SHORE DRIVE APARTMENTS TO SKIDMORE, OWINGS & MERRILL'S INLAND STEEL BUILDING.

construction–D. H. Burnham and Co.'s Reliance Building (1894), Mies van der Rohe's Illinois Institute of Technology (1940–1972), and SOM's John Hancock Center (1969) to name a few. While black-and-white photographs (almost always elevation shots) and line drawings similarly represent projects, they are also accompanied by lengthy, technical texts. If in *Chicago Architects* words were subordinate to imagery, in *100 Years* imagery is subordinate to text. Indeed, the uninterrupted run of text throughout the

100 Years catalogue visually reinforces the overarching continuity of a homogeneous historical argument. Between the two catalogue representations of similar periods, in almost identically-sized formats, the exhibitions graphically depict two opposing notions of architectural history, split along the lines of structure versus form, and space versus symbol.[18] The graphic strategies deployed also imply two tiers of audience: popular and genealogical (or personal/idiosyncratic) in the case of *Chicago Architects*, and more academic and historical (or encyclopedic/inevitable) in the case of *100 Years*.

TIMING

A chronology of events reveals that the publicity for the exhibitions began well before their Chicago openings. As early as nine months before either show opened in Chicago, and while applications for grants from the National Endowment for the Arts and the Graham Foundation were still being written, architecture critic and editor of the regional trade journal *Inland Architect* Nory Miller gave a sneak preview in an essay entitled "Reshaping the Map of Chicago Architecture" written for the tabloid *Chicago Daily News*. [19] According to Miller, Chicago's accepted architectural history conceived through the dominant expression of the structural frame was about to be turned upside down. Her article was one of the first trailers for the *Chicago Architects* show.

Next, *Chicago Architects* opened on the east coast, two months before it opened in Chicago, due to a postponed opening of *100 Years*. With both catalogues already released, a series of events instigated a cluster of reviews ahead of the show's anticipated Chicago opening. After the opening at the Arthur A. Houghton Jr. Gallery of the Cooper Union in New York on February 27, 1976,[20] which was organized by John Hejduk, there was a symposium at New York's Institute for Architectural and Urban Studies on the evening of March 1, 1976, and a later run at Harvard's Gund Hall in Boston (March 26–late April). There was also a publicity announcement published in the consumer magazine *House & Garden* as well as ongoing reports in the *Chicago Daily News* and a dedicated issue of Chicago's professional architecture journal *Inland Architect*, while reviews of the east coast exhibition were published in the *Chicago Sun-Times, Art in America,* and *The New York Times*.[21] This collection of reviews, essays, and notices, which appeared in tabloids, newspapers, magazines, and journals, amounted to nothing short of a media blitz spanning popular and consumer media, professional journals, and academic institutions.[22] A prolonged media event gave *Chicago Architects* much needed endorsement according to Tigerman, who later commented, "we knew we had to gain some credibility before it opened in Chicago. And we did."[23] When the exhibition did finally open at the Time-Life Building the evening before *100 Years* opened at the MCA just around the corner, it did so to great anticipation.[24]

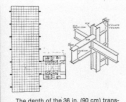

The depth of the 36 in. (90 cm) transverse girders, which carry openings for ducts, can be clearly read on the facade. The suspended ceiling is set back from the glass line and visually a clear distinction exists. The green-tinted sun control glass, contrary to the usual practice elsewhere, reaches from floor to ceiling—a characteristic of the Chicago school.

The separation of served and servant spaces, later elevated to a dogma by Louis Kahn, is in tall structures more tour de force than functional requirement, since it is more feasible economically to place vertical elements within the useable floor areas. Here they also serve as a portion of the wind bracing, and their position shortens the horizontal distances traversed by ducts and utilities.

For these reasons the floor plan organization of the Inland Steel Building remains an exception; the rule is, in Chicago, as elsewhere, to strive for high-rise buildings with the greatest allowable depth, and cores positioned as wind bracing in the middle zones.

The great spans and clear expression remain significant, and the shining stainless steel cladding and cantilevered end bays give the building a lightness which is in strong contrast to the weathering steel and bronze glazing of later buildings of the Chicago school.

Steel

Manhattan, New York

55

29

MANNER

Unsurprisingly, the publicity surrounding both exhibitions emphasized conflicting notions of history over curatorial format–indeed, very few articles featured photographs of either shows, which is surprising, but perhaps serves to underscore the rhetorical trumping of argument over evidence. [25] In nearly all of the reviews, which by April, 1976, were appearing in *Saturday Review, The New Art Examiner, Library Journal, Newsweek, The Nation,* and *Architectural Record,* the opposing arguments assumed the characteristics of a fight, a confrontation that was sensationalized in headlines like "Chicago's Design War" *(Chicago Daily News)*, "War of Ideas: Chicago's Battle of Architecture" *(Inland Architect)*, "Confrontation in Chicago" *(Saturday Review)*, "A Collision of Architectural Ideas" *(Chicago Tribune)*, and "Battle of the Buildings" *(Newsweek)*.[26] This populist casting of the architectural exchange transcended academic and professional criticism to find appeal in a public audience through popular media. Everyone, it seems, likes a good fight.

30 INSTALLATION VIEW, *CHICAGO ARCHITECTS*, PACIFIC DESIGN CENTER LOS ANGELES, 1977.

Beyond sensationalist headlines, the coverage of the exhibitions often amplified the juicy details. The *Chicago Daily News*, for example, anticipated the future opening of *Chicago Architects* in Chicago as "dogma-eat-dogma time," and forecasted "a head-on clash of ideas."[27] Quoting Tigerman for the *Chicago Daily News*, Miller reported that the show was "born in belligerence."[28] Paul Goldberger's *New York Times* review of the *Chicago Architects* exhibition at the Cooper Union described it as "an attack on architectural history"[29] while William Marlin's piece for the *Saturday Review* called it "a showdown" between "Miesian Sheriffs" and anti-Miesian "outlaws."[30] *Newsweek*'s Douglas Davis speculated that the controversy would "tear the safe, neat world of modern architecture completely apart,"[31] while Jane Holtz Kay in *The Nation* saw the debate as an "architectural war of the worlds."[32] When oral history interviewer Betty Blum asked Tigerman whether he and his colleagues saw the tension between the two exhibitions as the press portrayed it, Tigerman replied "Yep. We did."[33]

Indeed, it was Tigerman himself who "was looking for a fight" and who conceptualized the two exhibitions as a clash of epic proportions. [34] As a publicity tactic, this framing of conflicting notions of history allowed architectural ideas to be presented to a diverse audience in a riveting manner: the pro-con structure enabled ideas to be positioned within historical and conceptual frameworks; the sensation-alized tone engaged the popular absorption of ideas; and the productive spectacle diverted the local Chicago architectural conversation away from the pragmatics of

31 INSTALLATION VIEW, *100 YEARS OF ARCHITECTURE IN CHICAGO: CONTINUITY OF FORM AND STRUCTURE*, MCA CHICAGO, 1976.

building. In short, the catalogues, reviews, letters, and essays that surrounded both exhibitions amounted to a version of architectural culture that exceeded technology, practice, and buildings to embody a cultural discourse focused on spectacle, dis-agreement, and intellectual ideas, engaging the imaginative possibilities of a national and international audience across all genres of publication and styles of criticism. For Tigerman, the exhibition face-off demonstrated that "the world of ideas, not just the 'built environment,' is not quite yet dead in Chicago."[35]

CONTEXT

While the combative tone of the press coverage appealed to a broad audience, it did not preclude the disciplinary implications of the clash between the two exhibitions from being discussed in the same range of media too. While the east coast intelligentsia's perceived claim on architectural ideas had already been pointed out by Tigerman in his catalogue introduction, and again in a letter published in *Inland Architect* in which he claimed that "in the past only New York has supported the notion of architectural 'provocateurs' whereas Chicago buried them,"[36] the coverage of this notion did not stop there. Miller re-stated the problem in *Inland Architect*: "The mainstream to which *Chicago Architects* is addressing its 'me too' is not the mainstream of Chicago but the New York/Ivy League/trade press mainstream of the east coast." Here Miller was referring to New York's Whites and Grays, who for Miller constituted another kind of elite "no more open-mindedly pluralist than the structural imperative of the *100 Years* exhibit."[37] So, too, did architecture critic Paul Gapp, who noted in the *Chicago Tribune* that "the intellectual ballgame is played mostly in Manhattan, which holds a near-monopoly on the kinds of institutions, critics, and media that keep the conversation going."[38]

It was perhaps ironic, then, that it was the east coast architecture critic Ada Louise Huxtable who, in her *New York Times* review of *Chicago Architects* at the Cooper Union, laid out the broader disciplinary implications of the show and situated it in current concerns.[39] In her essay, entitled "Rediscovering Chicago Architecture," Huxtable situates the revisionist history of the counter-show in the context of emerging architectural interests in eclecticism. She writes: "This is fueling a revival of eclecticism, not as conventional academic borrowing, but as a means of image-making [...] This is why this kind of history so intrigues the present generation of practitioners; it is with a special eye that the past is being re-examined and, for better or worse, used in their own work. Today's eclecticism is a creative, cannibalistic combination of erudite nostalgia and extremely sophisticated aesthetics."[40] This revival of eclecticism, which had been consecutively raised from within the academy by Robert Venturi in *Complexity and Contradiction* (1966) and by Venturi, Denise Scott-Brown, and Steven Izenour in *Learning from Las Vegas* (1972), and later elaborated on in C. Ray Smith's *Supermannerism* (1977) and Charles Jencks's *The Language of Post-Modern Architecture* (1977), was a curatorial technique. By focusing precisely on a more inclusive and diverse history of Chicago's modern architecture and including the work of overlooked architects such as David Adler, Edward Dart, William Pereira, Andrew Rebori, and Howard Van Doren Shaw, the exhibition itself can be understood as an early engagement of an emerging architectural discourse on symbolism, eclecticism, and nascent historicist post-modernism but *from the other side* of architectural culture. In other words, the intellectual ambitions of *Chicago Architects* were consistent with, and no less significant, than those emerging from inside the academy. Furthermore, they were playing themselves out in a broader public sphere, a fact that Paul Goldberger alluded to in his essay for the *New York Times*: "the [counter] show is trying to do more than broaden history, it is trying to change our very view of architecture" at the moment when "the movement throughout the country is toward a more romantic, even hedonistic architecture."[41]

Regardless of content, and exactly because of a precise attention to format, timing, manner, and architectural ideas, the tension between the two shows spoke well to the general public as well as to narrower professional audiences. As Gapp remarked in the *Chicago Tribune*, "one need know only a little about architecture to understand the collision of ideas represented in the exhibitions, [...] these are also shows that anybody can enjoy, and they include much more than pictures of buildings you have seen repeatedly."[42] The fact that both exhibitions articulated, so clearly, architectural positions, that they could be so easily sensationalized by the press through the hyperbole of "war," offers lessons for how intellectuals and practitioners might make architectural ideas lucid and compelling to a general public.

In the current moment, when North American architectural discourse remains polarized between academic writing in theory/history journals, descriptive reportage in consumer magazines, the trade press, and blogs, and an all-too-often accommodation to the lowest common denominator in exhibition culture where themes such as "green design" do little more than pander to an already indoctrinated public, the *Chicago Architects* exhibition and the debate culture it instigated provides a counter-example for how history might pass through the terrains of academy, genre, and audience. Certainly it draws attention to the distinction between what historicist post-modernism was (an appeal to ideas by way of history), and what it *became* (a historical style sans ideas that would be appropriated by professional practitioners). The separation of history from practice, later paralleled in architectural exhibition culture in general and perhaps only after historicist post-modernism ran its course during the late 1980s as architectural exhibitions came to engage the "public" by focusing on popular solutions rather than intellectual provocations, has led to a deep disassociation between the academy and the real world. In this context, the *Chicago Architects* exhibition perhaps marks one of the last moments when practicing architects sought to leverage history for the ends of contemporary design practice, to cultivate an ambition for ideas and polemics, and to engage a wider audience for architectural debate.

33

In *Chicago Architects* one can see an opportunity for architectural thinkers to be understood as designers of history, fabricating narratives for the purposes of advancing ideas and gaining clients, projects, and commissions. While clearly neither history nor practice on their own is enough, combining them does not automatically succeed either as *100 Years* demonstrates–a dose of history with business as usual. Instead, a discipline founded on the ideological projection of new worlds needs to deploy *both* history and practice–and whatever else might come its way–opportunistically to its own ends with the ambition of producing surprising combinations that do not confirm well-rehearsed stories. One aspect of this integration is to understand the writing of history as a form of design; as a means to create the possibilities for new kinds of disciplinary work. Surely there are still lessons to be learned from that '70s show.

NOTES

I am indebted to Taber Wayne of Tigerman McCurry Architects and Stanley Tigerman for facilitating access to archival material, namely the "TigerClips" press clippings, director Sarah Herda and Sarah Rogers of the Graham Foundation for granting access to the "Chicago Architects" grant application, and Stuart Cohen for steering me toward possible sources of exhibition photographs. Earlier versions of this essay were presented at the 63rd Society of Architectural Historians Annual Meeting in Chicago, April 22, 2010, and at the conference "The Future of History" at the A. Alfred Taubman College of Architecture and Urban Planning, Ann Arbor, MI, April 1, 2011.

[1] Despite published credits, Stanley Tigerman and Stuart Cohen were the principal figures behind this exhibition. In an interview, Ben Weese claimed "the overall thing was Stuart and Stanley and they really put the ideas into the catalog together." See *Oral History of Benjamin Horace Weese*, interviewed by Annemarie van Roessel, p. 53. © 2001 The Art Institute of Chicago, used with permission. Larry Booth also deferred credit: "This was all Stanley's doing and he should take full credit for it [...]. We made a critical mass of architects, but Stanley did all the work and Stuart wrote the essay." See *Oral History of Laurence O. Booth*, interviewed by Annemarie van Roessel, p. 48. © 2000 The Art Institute of Chicago, used with permission.

[2] Stuart Cohen, *"Chicago Architects,"* in *Chicago Architects* (Chicago: The Swallow Press Inc., 1976), p. 12.

[3] For a lucid account of the differences between historicism and genealogy, see Craig Owens, "Philip Johnson: History, Genealogy, Historicism," in David Whitney and Jeffrey Kipnis, eds., *Philip Johnson: The Glass House* (New York: Pantheon Books, 1993), pp. 80-90.

[4] Stanley Tigerman, "Introduction: *'A Salon des Refusés',"* in *Chicago Architects* (Chicago: The Swallow Press Inc., 1976), p. 8.

[5] In a letter addressed to Ben Weese inviting him to submit material to *Chicago Architects*, Tigerman writes that the catalogue will contain short essays by historians "Colin Rowe, Norris Kelly Smith, Carl Condit and others." Letter, May 29, 1975. Ben Weese Papers, Box 34, Folder 24. Special Collections, The Art Institute of Chicago.

[6] Peter C. Pran, "Introduction to the American Exhibition" in Oswald W. Grube, Peter C. Pran and Franz Schulze, *100 Years of Architecture in Chicago: Continuity of Structure and Form* (Chicago: Follett Publishing Company, 1977), p. 9. First edition authored by Peter C. Pran and Franz Schulze in 1976.

[7] *Oral History of Stuart Earl Cohen*, interviewed by Betty J. Blum, p. 59. © 2000 The Art Institute of Chicago, used with permission.

[8] Ibid., p. 60.

[9] Craig Owens, "Philip Johnson: History, Genealogy, Historicism," p. 88.

[10] Cohen writes: "It may be true that the architecture of this period does not primarily concern the technology of frame construction or its aesthetic expression, but the inference that this is the sole criterion for the judgment of architecture, and that architecture that begins from other ideas did not occur in Chicago or was not influential, is myopic." See Stuart Cohen, "Chicago Architects," p. 11.

[11] Stanley Tigerman, National Endowment for the Arts grant application. General records corresponding to the grant for the architectural exhibition *Chicago Architects*, made to the Chicago School of Architecture

Foundation in 1975 under the directorship of Carter H. Manny. Archives of the Graham Foundation for Advanced Studies in the Fine Arts (Chicago, IL), Grant Files, 7543.

[12] The Chicago Seven consisted of Tigerman, Cohen, Ben Weese, Jack Hartray, Larry Booth, Tom Beeby, and Jim Nagle (and were sometimes expanded to include James Freed and Helmut Jahn).

[13] Stanley Tigerman, "Introduction: 'A Salon des Refusés,'" p. 8.

[14] Cohen explained: "When I came to Chicago, my sense was that there wasn't an architectural community, that there was a kind of vacuum. [...] It was a shock. I kept thinking, if you're passionate about architecture, don't you want to sit around and discuss ideas? Here was this kind of black, Miesian silence." *Oral History of Stuart Earl Cohen*, interviewed by Betty J. Blum, p. 52-53. © 2000 The Art Institute of Chicago, used with permission.

[15] Stanley Tigerman, "Introduction: 'A Salon des Refusés,'" p. 8.

[16] The Whites consisted of Peter Eisenman, Michael Graves, John Hejduk, Richard Meier, and Charles Gwathmey; the Grays of Robert Stern, Jack Robertson, Allan Greenberg, Charles Moore, and Ronaldo Giurgula.

[17] Stanley Tigerman, National Endowment for the Arts grant application. Archives of the Graham Foundation for Advanced Studies in the Fine Arts (Chicago, IL), Grant Files, 7543.

[18] Stuart Cohen, "Chicago Architects," p. 11.

[19] See Nory Miller, "Reshaping the Map of Chicago Architecture," *Panorama - Chicago Daily News* (August 16-17, 1975), p. 10.

[20] For a review of this symposium, see Nory Miller, "*Chicago Architects* the New Show in N.Y.," *Panorama - Chicago Daily News* (March 6-7, 1976), p. 13. Bertrand Goldberg, Monroe Bowman, Howard Fisher, Philip Johnson, Arthur Drexler (MoMA), Stuart Cohen, and Stanley Tigerman participated in this symposium.

[21] See, for example, Mike Reinhardt, "Chicago Architecture New View," *House & Garden* (February 1976), p. 14; "Wrapup: Chicago's Design War," *Panorama - Chicago Daily News* (February 28-29, 1976); Nory Miller, ed., *Inland Architect*, special issue (March 1976); Paul Goldberger, "A New Look at Chicago Architecture," *The New York Times* (March 4, 1976), p. 23; Nory Miller, "'Chicago Architects'- The New Show in N.Y.," *Panorama - Chicago Daily News* (March 6-7, 1976), p. 13; Ada Louise Huxtable, "Rediscovering Chicago Architecture," *The New York Times* (March 14, 1976), p. D30; Franz Schulze, "Architecture City: Two Views," *Art in America* (March-April, 1976), pp. 98-100; Nory Miller, "Building up a Battle of Buildings," *Panorama - Chicago Daily News* (April 24-25, 1976), pp. 2-3; and Rob Cuscaden, "Are Chicago's Architects in a Real War?" *Chicago Sun-Times* (April 25, 1976).

[22] Cohen later remarked: "Stanley made it, with some help from Nory [Miller], into a media event." *Oral History of Stuart Earl Cohen*, interviewed by Betty J. Blum, p. 67. © 2000 The Art Institute of Chicago, used with permission.

[23] *Oral History of Stanley Tigerman*, interviewed by Betty J. Blum, p. 139. © 2003 The Art Institute of Chicago, used with permission.

[24] Cohen remarked that the lobby of the Time-Life Building "was a silly place to put our show, except that Stanley was absolutely right to say that it was around the corner so people could see one and then just walk over and see the other one." *Oral History of Stuart Earl Cohen*, interviewed by Betty J. Blum, p. 67. © 2000 The Art Institute of Chicago, used with permission. *Chicago Architects* appeared in the Time-Life Building until June 20, 1976. After that, the exhibition traveled to other venues including the Illinois Institute of Technology (September 1976), UC Berkeley (October 1976), UCLA (November 1976), and The Pacific Design Center, Los Angeles (April 1977).

[25] The only published photograph of *Chicago Architects* I have come across appeared in the *Los Angeles Times* when the exhibition was held at the Pacific Design Center during April–May 1977. In this context and in a rare, brief review of the show's physical layout, the exhibition was criticized for being "tragically difficult to understand" and lacking in "continuity," perhaps the very historical continuity the show was trying to avoid. According to the *Los Angeles Times* architecture and design critic John Dreyfuss, these curatorial shortcomings obfuscated the important polemical message of *Chicago Architects*. See John Dreyfuss, "A Window on Chicago Architects," *Los Angeles Times* (April 26, 1977), p. G4. In contrast, Chicago's Museum of Contemporary Art does hold photographs of *100 Years* in its archive.

[26] See for example: William Marlin, "Confrontation in Chicago," *Saturday Review* (May 1, 1976), pp. 48–50; Paul Gapp, "A Collision of Architectural Ideas," *Chicago Tribune* (May 3, 1976), p. B3; "Show 1: 'Mavericks' on View at Time-Life Building," *Chicago Tribune* (May 3, 1976), p. E16; Paul Gapp, "Mies van der Rohe, Pro and Con: Two Shows Take a Stand," *Chicago Tribune* (May 23, 1976), p. E16; Paul Goldberger, "Two Views of Chicago-School Architects," *The New York Times* (June 1, 1976), p. 44; Jane Allen and Derek Guthrie, "City of Towers Exposed: Two Architecture Shows," *The New Art Examiner*, vol. 3, no. 9 (June 1976), np; H. Ward Jandl, "Chicago Architects," *Library Journal* (June 15, 1976), pp. 1409–1410; Irv Kupcinet, "Kup's column," *Chicago Sun-Times* (June 15, 1976), np; Margaret Carroll, "People," *Chicago Tribune* (June 20, 1976), p. 29; Douglas Davis, "Battle of the Buildings," *Newsweek* (June 21, 1976), pp. 85, 87; Jane Holtz Kay, "Architecture," *The Nation* (August 14, 1976), pp. 125–126; Richard B. Oliver, "A Tale of Two Cities," *Architectural Record* (September 1976), p. 43; Nory Miller, "Mining the Past, Eyes on Tomorrow," *Panorama - Chicago Daily News* (December 18–19, 1976), p. 19; "Exhibit Features Chicago Architects," *Los Angeles Times* (April 17, 1977), p. G2; and John Dreyfuss, "A Window on Chicago Architects," *Los Angeles Times* (April 26, 1977), p. G4–5.

[27] "Wrapup: Chicago's Design War," *Panorama - Chicago Daily News* (February 28, 1976), np.

[28] Nory Miller, "'Chicago Architects'- The New Show in N.Y.," *Panorama - Chicago Daily News*, (March 6–7, 1976), p. 13.

[29] Paul Goldberger, "A New Look at Chicago Architecture," *The New York Times* (March 4, 1976), p. 23.

[30] William Marlin, "Confrontation in Chicago," *Saturday Review* (May 1, 1976), pp. 48, 50.

[31] Douglas Davis, "Battle of the Buildings," *Newsweek* (June 21, 1976), p. 85.

[32] Jane Holtz Kay, "Architecture," *The Nation* (August 14, 1976), p. 125.

[33] *Oral History of Stanley Tigerman*, interviewed by Betty J. Blum, p. 140. © 2003 The Art Institute of Chicago, used with permission. For Cohen, however, the battle was less of a concern: "Stanley billed it as the Battle of the Titans. Where I would have done a quiet counter show, Stanley had everyone believing that this was a battle to the death between guys who painted their buildings black and guys who painted their buildings something else. The media, including the national architectural magazines, just bought it." See *Oral History of Stuart Earl Cohen*, interviewed by Betty J. Blum, p. 67. © 2000 The Art Institute of Chicago, used with permission. This style of coverage also generated dismissal by some who tried to play down "The Fight." For example, Chicago critic and co-organizer of the *100 Years* show, Franz Schulze, wrote in *Art in America*: "This is finally no confrontation at all, but rather a complementarity of perspectives that makes everybody's field of vision wider." Schulze later lamented in a letter published in *Inland Architect* that "the principal impression most people seem to have carried away from the two shows was of The Fight, followed at some distance by the issues behind The Fight, and more distantly still by the architecture the events presumably celebrated." See Franz Schulze, "Architecture City: Two Views," *Art in America* (March–April 1976), p. 100, and Franz Schulze, letter, *Inland Architect* (July 1976), p. 25. Co-organizer Peter C. Pran also declared in the *Saturday Review* that "there can really be no confrontation between the two shows [...]

the outlaws exhibit is certainly no challenge to the urban, architectural design shown in our exhibit."
Pran quoted in William Marlin, "Confrontation in Chicago," *Saturday Review* (May 1, 1976), p. 50.

[34] This was according to Larry Booth, who retrospectively remarked as well: "Stanley is a street-fighter and he was looking for a fight." See *Oral History of Laurence O. Booth*, interviewed by Annemarie van Roessel, p. 48. © 2000 The Art Institute of Chicago, used with permission.

[35] Stanley Tigerman, "Letter," *Inland Architect* (July 1976), p. 26.

[36] Ibid.

[37] Nory Miller, "War of Ideas: Chicago's Battle of Architecture," *Inland Architect* (March 1976), p. 14.

[38] Paul Gapp, "A Collision of Architectural Ideas," *Chicago Tribune* (May 3, 1976), p. B3.

[39] On the background, Cohen later explained: "Stanley again, in a very masterful way, made sure that catalogs got out there before the show opened and before we got there. He arranged a lunch with John Hejduk and Ada Louise Huxtable and both of us in the tower room of the Cooper Union building, where the works for the big clock are. We walked Ada Louise through the show and she seemed very interested and graciously accepted a catalog and then she was off. She did not attend the opening, which meant that the review of the show was written from her ten-minute walk-through and the catalog. All of the visual images from the show were in the catalog. Stanley was smart about that because the catalog remains after the show is taken down and it is ultimately the lasting reason for doing the show."
Oral History of Stuart Earl Cohen, interviewed by Betty J. Blum, p. 79. © 2000 The Art Institute of Chicago, used with permission.

[40] Ada Louise Huxtable, "Rediscovering Chicago Architecture," *The New York Times* (March 14, 1976), p. D30.

[41] Paul Goldberger, "Two Views of Chicago-School Architects," *The New York Times* (June 1, 1976), p. 44.

[42] Paul Gapp, "A Collision of Architectural Ideas," *Chicago Tribune* (May 3, 1976), p. B3.

THE PORTFOLIO AS ARCHITECTURAL MATERIAL

The 1910 publication *Ausgeführte Bauten und Entwürfe von Frank Lloyd Wright*, today known as the Wasmuth Folio, is a monster. It is simultaneously a record of modern architecture's deliberate self-invention, -declaration, and -promotion, and an incomparable demonstration of modern architecture's unexpected, accidental mutation into a world of knowledge and experience defined by architecture's increasingly mediated forms of information and communication. Created as a projectile for both re-launching Wright's career and ushering in his exit from Chicago's Oak Park, the staggering international success of the Wasmuth Folio was groundbreaking for another reason entirely: its systematic invention of a wholly new kind of modern building material: the architectural monograph. As Wasmuth's success in sending Wright's project well beyond the horizon of Lake Michigan testifies, the modern architectural monograph and its influence in declaring, promoting, and communicating architectural ideas would matter more than any other material in changing architecture's fortune in the twentieth century.

Conceived as a series of one hundred large-format drawings and published as a table-smothering folio of the same size, the Wasmuth Folio contained only drawings made in Wright's studio "after the fact" of his buildings' completion. In this sense the folio is a remarkable catalogue of the studio itself, with its means of representation, communication, and vision nearly identical in portfolio form to the memorable compositions; and plans, views, cutaway sections, and elevations on each plate coordinated with masterful drafting room techniques. This original, first edition would later evolve into the familiar coffee table format of more recent architectural monographs, from Mies's 1946 MoMA book, to Philip Johnson's gold-foil, color-photo record in the 1960s, Richard Meier's Vignelli-designed white book a decade later, and Koolhaas and Mau's genre-killing *S,M,L,XL* of 1995. Wasmuth's definitive conception of this genealogy was made even more complex when a year later the same Berlin publisher re-released the material as a small-format booklet of photographs and simplified plans, forever ending the nineteenth-century drafting-room impulse that had driven the creation of this modern masterpiece.

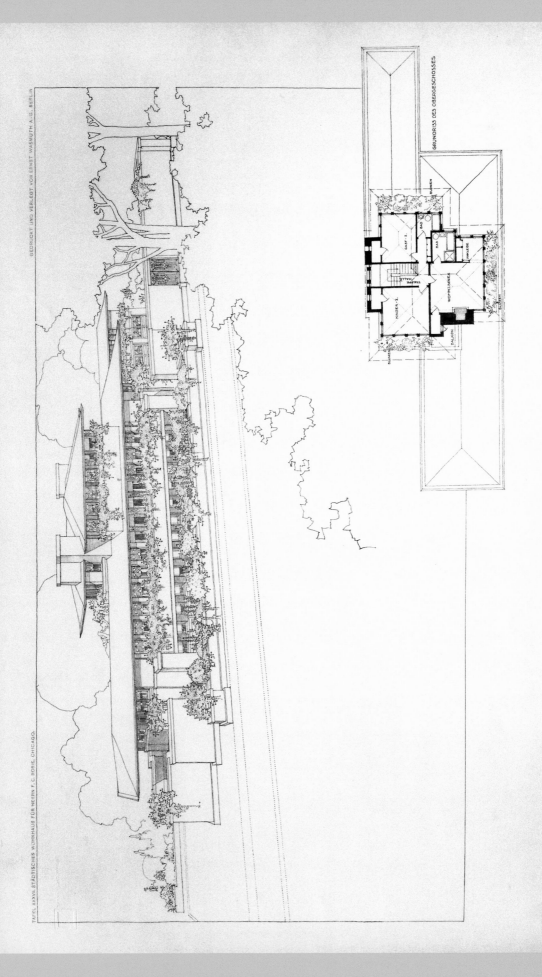

GRUNDRISS DES OBERGESCHOSSES

TAFEL XXXVII. STÄDTISCHES WOHNHAUS FÜR HERRN F. C. ROBIE, CHICAGO.

GEDRUCKT UND VERLEGT VON ERNST WASMUTH A.-G. BERLIN

WASMUTH FOLIO. FRANK LLOYD WRIGHT, 1910.

PERVERTED MONUMENT

SAM JACOB

Though Adolf Loos's Chicago Tribune Tower was never built, it weighs heavy on our architectural imagination. The image of its black marble Doric column scaled to the size of a skyscraper remains both dumb and provocative. This cyclopean piece of decoration is all the stranger coming from the author of *Ornament and Crime*, that spiky *cri de coeur* against decoration. But perhaps the essay and proposal are not so different after all. Both are manifestoes, provocations taking textual and architectural form in turn.

When reading Loos's Tribune Tower as though it were text, its form becomes an intentionally bad joke: a news-paper column monumentalized as a newspaper office. It plays with symbols, definitions, and expectations as it looks like a column but holds nothing up, inverts the traditional white Grecian marble into shiny black, and, most of all, inverts Loos's own position as set out in *Ornament and Crime*. Instead of having "gone beyond ornament" with "plain, undecorated simplicity," he gives us an ornament *ne pas ultra*. While huge, it is also like a Bakelite object that would sit on a desk in an office.

The Tribune Tower is the most austere of ornaments – not something comforting but an aggressive challenge. Loos's Tribune Tower is dark; not just in color but in tone. Its perversity and irony can only be read as a sarcastic gift to the cultural hobgoblins the author describes in *Ornament and Crime*, as critique-by-fulfillment of an architectural culture that he stood against. Loos saw his Tribune Tower as an inevitable product of the culture he witheringly despised. He wrote: "The great Greek Doric column must be built. If not in Chicago, then in some other town. If not for the 'Chicago Tribune' then for some-one else. If not by me, then by some other architect." The Tribune Tower may be utterly perverse, yet through its utter deviancy, Loos delivers the purest of architectural critiques, wrapped up in an indelible architectural image.

CHICAGO TRIBUNE TOWER PROJECT, ADOLF LOOS, 1922.

ALVIN BOYARSKY'S CHICAGO-LONDON AXIS

AN ARCHITECTURAL CRITIC IN THE CITY OF STRANGERS

IGOR MARJANOVIĆ

I learned a rather nice word the other day from an American anthropologist: culture shock. It's what Zulus get when they come to London or the English when they go to Iowa. My dear Elizabeth you are destined to suffer from it all your life. You had it in Montreal, in Ithaca, now in Eugene, and you will have it just as badly when you get back to London. COLIN ROWE, IN A LETTER TO ELIZABETH AND ALVIN BOYARSKY, 1960.

Colin Rowe wrote these words [1] to his friends Elizabeth Boyarsky, an English compatriot, and her Canadian husband Alvin, an architecture professor in distant Eugene, Oregon, responding to their anxiety of living in a small college town in the American Northwest. Rowe had met the young couple in 1957 while teaching at Cornell University, where Boyarsky was a graduate student in urban planning. His words reflect a close friendship and affection born out of Sunday brunches and dinner parties in upstate New York. But they also suggest a shared dislocation wrought by their constant transatlantic moves and culture shocks. For Rowe, these moves included his teaching experience in both the UK and the US and Boyarsky made similar transatlantic crossings:

43 ALVIN BOYARSKY AT A SIT-IN FOR CAMBODIA, UNIVERSITY OF ILLINOIS AT CHICAGO-CIRCLE, MAY 1970.

he was born and raised in Montreal in a family of Jewish immigrants from Eastern Europe; he then practiced architecture in London in the 1950s, where he met his wife, only to come back to North America, first as a student at Cornell (1957–1959) and later as a professor in Eugene, Oregon (1959–1962). He then taught in London (1962–1965), followed by a stint in Chicago (1965–1972), finally returning to London to lead the Architectural Association School of Architecture (1971–1990). While his chairmanship at the AA launched a number of novel ideas and discourses, including the practices of Zaha Hadid, Rem Koolhaas, and Bernard Tschumi, just to name a few, his Chicago episode offers important insight into the larger cultural shifts that seeded later architectural currents at the AA.

Despite his Canadian origins, Boyarsky adopted a rather European lifestyle through his lived experience in London and his admiration for Italian urbanism. Consecrating this shared affection, Rowe and Boyarsky traveled to Italy together in 1964, where they encountered a newly wed couple–Peter Eisenman and his English wife Elisabeth. Through these encounters, and their subsequent, increasingly mythologized retelling, a diasporic picture emerges of traveling architects, displaced strangers, and a cross-cultural fertilization in which Boyarsky was very obviously at home; or as Rowe put it, "a certain condition of elegant Jewish wit at Cornell, highly intelligent, highly Italianate and determined to observe things Italian from an American perspective."[2] Rowe encountered this "American perspective" while mentoring Boyarsky's dissertation on Camillo Sitte, a late-nineteenth-century Viennese architect who rejected modern progressivism. Scholars such as Rudolf Wittkower, Rowe's mentor, had already rediscovered Sitte, and Boyarsky's study certainly extended that trajectory–he commended Sitte's contextualism and pragmatism, echoing Rowe's writings and his pedagogical work at the University of Texas at Austin as a member of the so-called Texas Rangers that sought to re-contextualize and historicize modern architecture.[3] Yet, Boyarsky's dissertation "Camillo Sitte: City Builder," added a new angle to this scholarship by examining the reception of Sitte's Italianate ideas in the Anglo-Saxon world.[4]

Indeed, this cross-cultural translation reveals Boyarsky's own oscillation between his "American perspective" and his desire for a European lifestyle–a dilemma captured in his correspondence with Rowe, who advised Boyarsky not to come to the UK.[5] Boyarsky, however, moved to London in 1962, only to experience firsthand the alienation within British academia that Rowe had warned him about.[6] By early 1965, he became aware of a job opening at the University of Illinois at Chicago-Circle, a new architecture school looking for a faculty member and an associate for Dean Leonard Currie, a former student of Walter Gropius. After the job interview, Boyarsky visited Rowe in upstate New York, where he shared his fascination for Chicago. Although Rowe persuaded him to take the job, the eventual move to Chicago was also a beginning of a separation between the two.[7] "Chicago was a major event in my life," he recalled, "I became interested in a different path really through the fact of Chicago."[8] This "different path" marks a shift in Boyarsky's scholarship from Rowe's historicist focus to a more eclectic set of urban and social issues–issues that so powerfully resonated in Chicago when Boyarsky arrived there in summer 1965.

44

CHICAGO AS A NEW BEGINNING

Initially Dean Currie wanted only an assistant, but once he saw Boyarsky's potential he elevated the post to an associate deanship with tenure. Boyarsky rose to the occasion, translating the city's political radicalism of the 1960s into new ideas about pedagogy and historiography. As a critic he continued to write and talk about contemporary architects in venues that ranged from architectural periodicals to appearances in BBC documentaries.[9] As the associate dean, Boyarsky focused on everyday operations, including the budget and room and teaching schedules, yet the responsibility for the social life of the school slowly emerged as his main preoccupation. He became obsessed with lecture series, symposia, and social events. He threw parties at his apartment and seeded a lasting relationship with the neighboring Italian and Greek restaurants, which became extensions of the school itself–an idea of the restaurant as school later mastered at the AA and nearby Charlotte Street.

Yet this social scene was shaken by Chicago's turbulent political context, which permeated Boyarsky's teaching strategies. Jack Naughton, his former Chicago student, remembered: "Those years were volatile; fraught with desires for social change. I remember my admiration for Alvin and his ability as a teacher to both feed our idealism with contemporary possibilities and temper our potential zealotry with questions of responsibility."[10] This ability to manage the energy of young people was fully tested during the campus protests in May 1970 following the Kent State Massacre. Students stormed the university requesting the closure of all buildings and the termination of all teaching activities. Dean Currie was in South America and so Boyarsky assumed full responsibility for the fragile situation. Unlike other administrators, however, he decided to work with the students and to make the school available to protesters, becoming in the process the main negotiator between students and the university.

He strategically opened the UIC architecture building as the "headquarters" of student activities–the only open building on campus where students both protested and worked. The protesters first rejected this idea, but later agreed to Boyarsky's limited terms–"everyone must be out at 1 am."[11] And so Walter Netsch's oddly shaped and windowless building, unfinished even to this day, became a centre of dialogue, relaxing the tensions on campus. As Boyarsky wrote to Rowe, "Netsch's crystal geometry" became "an all-happening, electronically geared, graphically revolting communication center," a "guerilla theater" and a hub for "the propaganda business."[12] Boyarsky's management of the situation earned him support from the upper administration. It also empowered him with a revolutionary zeal that he hoped could change the school: "We hope to do our bit by channeling the students' energies and upsetting the static curricula and unthinking activities of so many of the staff. [...] The motto universally is FUCK NIXON and more locally, Build People. Not Buildings."[13]

But such political activism was at odds with Chicago's architectural culture. UIC was a divided community comprising two very different groups: the locals and the foreigners. The foreign contingent included a Swiss group–Niklaus Morgenthaler, Jacques Blumer, and Peter Gygax–as well as Graeme Morland from Scotland and Boyarsky. The domestic contingent included local practitioners deeply engrained in the professional culture of the Midwest. The intellectualism of the foreigners contrasted with the corporate professionalism of the locals. Stanley Tigerman recalled:

Boyarsky was here in Chicago and he was trying to do something in the presence of anti-intellectualism that still exists today. [...] Boyarsky was the only guy in a position of any authority who was an intellectual, theoretically inclined, and very smart. [...] But we all treated him badly, to my recollection [...]. There may have been exceptions. Maybe, Niklaus Morgenthaler and other visiting critics were nicer to him. The locals saw him as a kind of foreign reserve contingent.[14]

46 ALVIN BOYARSKY (MIDDLE) DURING CAMPUS PROTESTS, UNIVERSITY OF ILLINOIS AT CHICAGO-CIRCLE, MAY 1970.

This intellectualism and internationalism were also recognized by Peter Blake, editor of *Architectural Forum*, who called Boyarsky "an architect and critic who is genuinely interested in education," and "aware of all that is going on in this country and abroad."[15] Boyarsky's intellectual distance from Chicago's academic and professional establishments allowed him to transform the school into an environment of ideas, exchange, and protest, uninhibited by structured curriculum or corporate office cultures. This discursiveness was clearly at odds with UIC's practical ambition of producing practitioners for the city's big offices – a form of social mobility that occurred in the context of constant political riots embattled with tear gas grenades.

For the Boyarsky family, living in a North Side apartment, the smell of tear gas was all too familiar.[16] Yet they continued with their European lifestyle, always walking or catching public transport and never owning a car. The family's lack of a vehicle suggests a temporariness to their stay in Chicago, and despite Boyarsky's intellectual interest in the city's radicalism, Rowe claimed that the couple grew increasingly anxious due to the city's high crime rates.[17] A pedestrian stranger in a car society, Boyarsky nevertheless developed an intellectual affection for the city that became an inspiration for new ways of writing history and new forms of pedagogy. This "fact of Chicago," as he had called it, could be seen as a dual metaphor of "Chicago as Catalyst" and "Chicago as Pedagogy" – a conceptual framework of inherent conflicts, ambiguities, and politics that powerfully resurfaced in texts and educational experiments that Boyarsky soon developed.

CHICAGO AS CATALYST

The image of Boyarsky as a pedestrian observer of Chicago appeared in 1966 in Chicago's *American Magazine*, where he offered a walking tour of the city's architectural icons: Bertrand Goldberg's Marina City, he said, "adds excitement," and Frank Lloyd Wright's Robie House is "warm and friendly." But gradually, he diverted the conversation into a broader context. Acting as a social critic, he attacked the city's "bleak" public housing projects. He projected the misery of public housing through children who had to "travel from a twelve-story apartment to the ground in order to play," reflecting the personal concerns of a father and an estranged Sittesque pedestrian.[18]

Eventually, these observations grew into more frequent contributions to *Architectural Design*, culminating in his 1970 special issue on Chicago, which featured his essay "Chicago *à la Carte:* The City as an Energy System" based on his collection of picture postcards.[19] The use of postcards was not coincidental: as traveling ephemera, the postcard mirrored Boyarsky's peripatetic living arrangements, reflecting also his passion for collecting. From china and rugs to aerial photographs, his collecting passion was contagious, with friends quickly succumbing to it – notably Rowe, who accompanied Boyarsky on trips to the Oriental rug market in Chicago.[20] Boyarsky's collections also included newspaper clippings and political posters of Black Panthers and campus protests, as well as vintage and contemporary postcards of Chicago. An active deltiologist in Chicago, Boyarsky was a member of the Windy City Postcard Club. Gathered from Chicago airports, antique shops, and flea markets, his postcards depict grain elevators, canals, slaughterhouses, railroads, bridges, and airports, all intertwined with images of parks, landmarks, and public works, with very few postcards of buildings designed by master architects.[21]

"Chicago *à la Carte*" weaved together this imagery with Boyarsky's own captions and borrowed quotations, reflecting his unique writing style – endless sen-

47

tences, the hoarding of words, images and maps. With its diverse visual evidence, the essay is a study in the site-specificity that Boyarsky had already assigned to Sitte as a "constant revision and change to meet evolving social and political conditions."[22] Boyarsky borrowed these ideas consciously–the essay was meant to grow into a book-long study *City Building: Strategies and Satires.*[23] While the title paraphrases Sitte's book, the subtitle revealed an inherent tension in his methodology–"strategies" spoke to an empirical architect-planner and social commentator, while "satires" paved the way for Boyarsky's more impassioned personal observations.

The postcards were liberating, as they were relieved of "historical continuity and purely compositional activities involving good taste, harmony and delicacy of expression."[24] *"Chicago à la Carte"* reads like a travel documentary, echoing some of the earlier traveling ruminations of Rowe and Sitte, who also collected distant vistas, displacing their image collections into the world of architectural historiography. But unlike their romanticized vision of Italy, Boyarsky offered a complex image of America

"oozing with caricature."[25] Yet, he maintained a highly critical voice–"Chicago is only half a city," he lamented, referring to its abrupt ending by the lake, but also to its racial divide.[26] Dismayed by the city's public housing, he advocated for public-private partnerships such as Goldberg's Marina City, a popular icon of its time. A *Chicago Daily News* reporter wrote in 1964: "People who sell postcards tell me they sell more illustrating this unique piece of modern architecture than any other Chicago view."[27] Boyarsky, too, published its postcard, praising its "extraordinary section" that revealed "the grittiness and complexity of Chicago's multilayered infrastructure."[28] This layered building section is one of the recurring themes in the essay, starting from the cover page, showing the State Street section with different forms of underground and surface transportation.

Reaffirming his role as a social critic, Boyarsky contrasted Chicago's contemporary architecture with its politics, juxtaposing images of the July 1970 riots to the Sears Tower. The short headlines from the *Chicago Tribune* captured the paradox, "A Thousand Storm Loop"; "Sears to Construct Tallest Building in World."[29] Nowhere was this evolving social dynamic more visible than at O'Hare International Airport, the embodiment of affordable air travel and new technology. Yet, its environmental impact was grim–an important ethical concern that prompted Boyarsky to think ahead of his time. "One jet liner arriving or taking off at O'Hare spews as much pollution in the air as 72 cars operating full blast for 20 minutes [...] each plane pours 29 pounds of hydrocarbons in the air," he wrote in his notes.[30] The airport's public function was

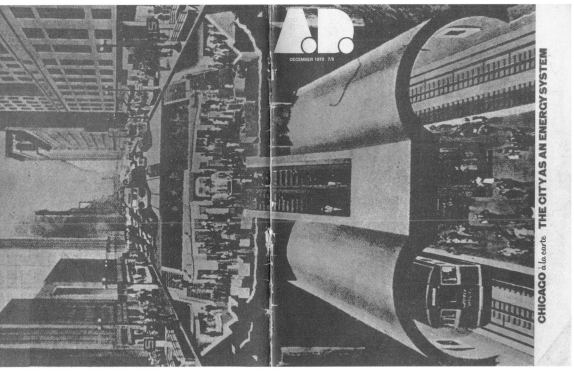

49   COVER OF *ARCHITECTURAL DESIGN*, DECEMBER 1970.

also highly questionable–"O'Hare, Versailles to Chicago, is where only the rich can circulate."[31] An illustration in the essay exposes that commoditization–a "flying man" with gadgets, an icon of middle-class empowerment in the image of a white man. As much as O'Hare was a powerful symbol of social and environmental debasement, it also offered intriguing architectonic parallels with the city itself: its layered sectional diagram recalled Chicago's infrastructure.

O'Hare was also, in many ways, the closest thing that Boyarsky had to a home. Through endless trips between the Midwest and Europe, it is easy to imagine him spending a large amount of time in its terminal buildings, surrounded by "the smell of infra red cooking (Vermont Ham, Maryland Chicken, Florida Snapper) and distant pastoral scenes (Mount Rushmore, Death Valley, the Plains of Texas) as well as groomed stewardesses [...]."[32] This image of an architect sitting in an airport building, writing notes to himself in a stream of consciousness, both appalled and attracted by the visual and sonic cacophony around him, would re-emerge in Rem Koolhaas's "Junkspace"– a text so close to Boyarsky's own as to appear almost as an homage.[33] OMA's early aesthetic thrived on visual disjunction and was often predicated on the postcard. Koolhaas observed, "Alvin probably influenced to some degree my subconscious," mostly through his "lack of sentimentality" and "the evident pleasure with which he discussed dangerous situations in architecture."[34] This is particularly evident in Koolhaas's *Delirious New York*, where postcards of Coney Island are used to fuse media and spectacle in architecture.[35] And like Koolhaas's terminal meditations, Boyarsky's endless sentences recall a postcard depiction–an impromptu "airport philosophy" derived from constant of travel.

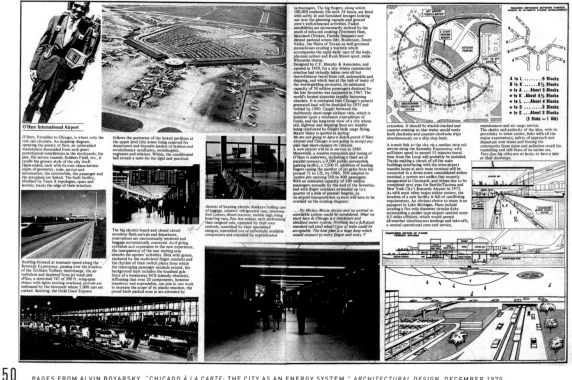

50   PAGES FROM ALVIN BOYARSKY, "CHICAGO À LA CARTE: THE CITY AS AN ENERGY SYSTEM," *ARCHITECTURAL DESIGN*, DECEMBER 1970.

Boyarsky offers no resistance to this condition; instead he sharpens our appreciation for everyday spaces of North American cities, including Chicago's Merchandise Mart, once the world's largest commercial building and "a masterpiece of junk culture."[36] This "city as a building," as Boyarsky had called it, mirrors Koolhaas's "bigness," where beyond a certain critical mass a building becomes a city in itself.[37] Boyarsky's essay examines many such buildings, including Chicago's main post office that "swallowed" the Eisenhower Expressway, praising their bold connection to the city's infrastructure and economy. Yet, as the essay draws to a close, it eludes a clear conclusion. Instead, the violent images of political protests gradually replace the everyday nobility of the postcard, charging the essay with implied social criticism.

CHICAGO AS PEDAGOGY

Empowered by O'Hare to operate on a transatlantic basis, Boyarsky soon launched the International Institute of Design (IID) Summer Sessions in London that brought together participants from around the world.[38] Conceived from his Chicago base during the school year, the six-week-long Summer Sessions were Boyarsky's independent operation during his summer breaks from UIC. The first IID session was hosted by The Bartlett in 1970, while the AA and the Institute of Contemporary Arts in Pall Mall accommodated the next two sessions. Envisioned as a series of problem-based workshops and lectures, they involved numerous architects and critics including the members of Archigram, James

STAMPS FOR THE 1970 INTERNATIONAL INSTITUTE OF DESIGN SUMMER SESSION DESIGNED BY SAMPSON/FETHER.

Stirling, Hans Hollein, Colin Rowe, Robin Middleton, Cedric Price, Reyner Banham, and many others. The students could choose from a number of workshops, interacting with a series of rotating faculty, whose portraits were featured on the IID postcards and stamps.

The IID promoted cross-cultural dialogue in opposition to professional education constrained by licensure, standardization, and parochialism.[39] An environment of discourse, much like Boyarsky's student headquarters at UIC, it tackled issues from preservation to post-industrial site reclamation–themes already developed in *"Chicago à la Carte,"* which called "for the reclamation of many redundant networks of the tartan field."[40] With its polyphony of voices and images, the essay could also be read as a formal precedent not only for IID's ephemera of postcards, stamps, and posters; rather, its menu of floating postcards was appropriated as a *carte du jour* of IID's rolling workshops, lectures, and debates. The IID was "a market-place for ideas and a forum, a workshop and a platform, and operated as a well-laid table and banquet for free-ranging souls as opposed to the local cafeteria's battery fare."[41] Indeed, the *à la carte* menu patented in the Chicago essay became perfected in the "well-laid table" of the IID. In these words we see a reflection of the complex context of the early 1970s–while the "well-laid table" certainly mirrors the multiplicity of architectural discourses of the emerging post-modern era, it also echoes the diverse menu of images and voices from "Chicago à la Carte." [42] Yet, the "market-place" refers to an acceptance of economic flows–a form of pragmatism that imbued Boyarsky's Chicago scholarship and adminis-

POSTCARD FOR THE 1970 INTERNATIONAL INSTITUTE OF DESIGN SUMMER SESSION DESIGNED BY SAMPSON/FETHER.

trative experience: while handed political crises at UIC, he also recognized the importance of the city's economic foundations in "Chicago *à la Carte.*"

And just as "Chicago *à la Carte*" rejected the conventions of the scholarly essay, the IID rejected institutionalism and professionalism, embracing instead discourse and communication. To promote this ideal and the sessions themselves, an IID publishing blitz went into effect. It comprised posters, maps, brochures, and postcards, reflecting the discursiveness and popular sensibility of "Chicago *à la Carte.*" For example, the

"Manhattan Workshop Briefing Document" prepared by Archigram for the 1972 Summer Session focused on New York City's post-industrial sites, and offered a combination of empirical planning data and personal narratives told through newspaper clippings, maps, and planning documents. This eclectic publishing format foreshadowed Boyarsky's later publishing endeavors at the AA, as well as the work of AA notables such as Koolhaas's *Delirious New York* and Bernard Tschumi's *Manhattan Transcripts*.

Through IID Boyarsky also shifted from the collection of postcards to their production. In a postcard for the 1971 Summer Session, we see simultaneous dinner table conversations. A busy restaurant scene, it reflects Boyarsky's ideal of education as "a well-laid table"–a metaphor of pedagogical discursiveness and relative freedom of choice later perfected through the AA's unit system. This image was also a metaphor for Boyarsky's own management style–he self-directed the IID from London and Chicago through improvisation and networking. As he himself described, "I used to sit in my bathrobe at the kitchen table in Chicago and call Moscow, you know, and do things."[43]

POSTCARD FOR THE 1971 INTERNATIONAL INSTITUTE OF DESIGN SUMMER SESSION DESIGNED BY SAMPSON/FETHER.

Stretched between his apartment kitchen and the terminal building, he was assisted by Elizabeth and their two children, who stuffed envelopes with promotional materials. But the IID operation was truly global–students and "faculty" came from all over the world–an idea of travel clearly depicted in the official letterhead for the 1972 Summer Session, showing a soaring jet liner.

This image is powerful as it speaks to Boyarsky's pragmatic approach to building an international school empowered by an enhanced global flow of people and capital, but also to seeding it with an environmental discourse that deals with the critique of such capital. These issues are evident in some of the Summer Session themes such as historic preservation and community action (Covent Garden Workshop, 1971) and the industrial reclamation site (Manhattan Workshop, 1972). Multiplied several times, the jet on the IID logo suggests not only the reverberation of multiple voices of IID's international cadre of participants, but also Boyarsky's own simultaneous transatlantic roles – director of the IID, associate dean at UIC and, as of September 1971, chairman of the AA. "I don't have a base," he wrote, "I move around the world and so I always think of my activities as being involved with international events."[44] Boyarsky wanted to continue with this international operation through a post in Chicago that would allow him to work globally. Ultimately, however, he resigned after UIC rejected his application for a part-time tenure position. Thus, his attempt to operate on a Chicago-London axis failed, and with it an effort to institutionalize his foreignness.

CITIES OF STRANGERS

Chicago left a lasting mark on Boyarsky – Dennis Crompton called Boyarsky the "Chicago street fighter," referring to his improvisational skills picked up in Chicago and later deployed in London.[45] Yet, Boyarsky often described himself as an "alchemist" or "rainmaker," someone who quietly operates between the airport terminal and his own kitchen table, constantly making virtues out of necessities.[46] At UIC, he transformed the inflamed campus into a place of dialogue while at the AA, he turned the lack of studio space into a kind of brand. This displacement of the AA's studio production echoed Boyarsky's own condition and worked particularly well for international students, who were already displaced.[47] When the British government withdrew funding for UK students at the AA, he skillfully turned to the international market of students and faculty. This lasting internationalism had its roots in Boyarsky's own background, but also in his time spent in Chicago. What began as an affinity with the UIC's "Swiss contingent" grew into an international network of collaborators that he sustained well into his tenure at the AA. Like his Chicago dinner parties, the AA under Boyarsky was full of émigrés who, for the first time, became the leaders of an international architectural debate. It was a well-laid table, a platform, forum, and market-place – a series of metaphors often used by Boyarsky as synonyms for the word he despised the most: curriculum. "I've always felt that curriculum is a horrific thing," he wrote, "the opposite of that is a kind of anarchy – which I believe in wholeheartedly."[48]

This reference to anarchy reveals not only the past experience of UIC's protest-ridden campus, but perhaps inherent contradictions in Boyarsky's work – a trained architect and historian, who was familiar with academic hierarchies yet embraced popular culture, and a born traveler, who eventually spent almost twenty years in residence as the AA's chairman. These contradictions empowered Boyarsky to assume multiple roles, which enabled him to effectively speak to the students, encouraging them to "introduce a political note to their work"[49] that can tackle the establishment and polarize opinion. This was perhaps a lesson of Chicago's peculiar moment, where discursive campus protests and texts later resurfaced as polemical projects in London, promoting a form of creative strangeness that blossomed in the studios, books, and events that Boyarsky seeded.

This material was first presented at the 2010 Annual Meeting of the Society of Architectural Historians, in a session titled "Chicago in the World," chaired by Alexander Eisenschmidt and Jonathan Mekinda. It was initially published as Igor Marjanović, "Alvin Boyarsky's Chicago: An Architectural Critic in the City of Strangers," AA Files, no. 60 (Spring 2010): pp. 45–60, and is featured here in an abridged and revised version. I am indebted to Thomas Weaver, Alexander Eisenschmidt, and Jonathan Mekinda for their editorial input, as well as Nicholas and Nicola Boyarsky for facilitating my archival work in London.

[1] Letter from Colin Rowe to Al (Alvin) and Elizabeth Boyarsky, October 24, 1960, courtesy of the Alvin Boyarsky Archive, London (ABA).

[2] Colin Rowe, "Alvin Boyarsky: A Memory," in Alexander Caragonne, ed., *As I Was Saying: Recollections and Miscellaneous Essays*, vol. 3: Urbanistics (Cambridge, MA: MIT Press, 1996), p. 332.

[3] See Alexander Caragonne, *The Texas Rangers: Notes from an Architectural Underground* (Cambridge, MA: MIT Press, 1995).

[4] In his Master's Thesis, Boyarsky writes that Rowe was instrumental in his selection of the topic. The dissertation was developed under the supervision of Professor K. C. Pearson. See Alvin Simon Boyarsky, "Camillo Sitte: City Builder," thesis for the Degree of Master of Regional Planning (Ithaca, NY: Cornell University, September 1959), p. iii. Also mentioned in Colin Rowe, "Alvin Boyarsky: A Memory," p. 336.

[5] Letter from Colin Rowe to Alvin and Elizabeth Boyarsky, September 14, 1958, ABA.

[6] Between 1962 and 1965, Boyarsky taught at the Bartlett School of Architecture and at the Architectural Association, where he argued with the school's principal William Allen, a staunch modernist interested in empirical building science, over the nature of architectural education and was forced to leave the school.

[7] Colin Rowe, "Alvin Boyarsky: A Memory," p. 339.

[8] From an interview given to the AA Graduate School in 1974, ABA.

[9] For Boyarsky's discussion of Sir Denys Lasdun's Royal College of Physicians Building, see Alvin Boyarsky, "The Architecture of Etcetera," *Architectural Design* (June 1965), pp. 268–270. For Boyarsky's discussion of James Stirling, see Alvin Boyarsky, "Stirling *Dimostrationi*," *Architectural Design* (October 1968), pp. 454–455. In 1966, BBC 1 broadcast ten weekly documentaries titled *Masterbuilders*. An architectural critic prepared each episode. Boyarsky focused on Le Corbusier in an episode titled "Towards an Architecture." Other speakers included Joseph Rykwert, Reyner Banham, Robert Furneaux-Jordan, and Robin Middleton. See Alvin Boyarsky, "Towards an Architecture," in John Donat, ed., *Masterbuilders* (London: BBC, 1996), p. 5, ABA.

[10] Letter from Jack Naughton to Victoria Boyarsky, February 13, 1992, ABA.

[11] "Behind the Scenes of Circle Shutdown," *Chicago Illini* (May 7, 1970).

[12] Letter from Alvin Boyarsky to Colin Rowe, May 12, 1970, ABA.

[13] Ibid.

[14] Stanley Tigerman, in conversation with the author, August 10, 2005.

[15] In 1969, after Robert Geddes decided not to take on the deanship at Harvard University's Graduate School of Design, Peter Blake recommended Boyarsky to the then dean, José Luis Sert. See memo from Peter Blake to José Luis Sert, April 22, 1969, Harvard University Archives, Cambridge, MA. I am grateful to Eric Mumford for this source.

[16] Alvin and Elizabeth Boyarsky's children, Nicholas and Victoria, were born in the US.

[17] Colin Rowe, "Alvin Boyarsky: A Memory," p. 339.

[18] Richard Hoffmann, "Chicago: Study in Power and Clarity (a conversation with Alvin Boyarsky)," *Chicago's American Magazine*, January 9, 1966.

[19] Alvin Boyarsky, "Chicago *à la Carte*," *Architectural Design* (December 1970), pp. 595–640. Reprinted in Robin Middleton, ed., *Architectural Associations: The Idea of the City* (Cambridge, MA: MIT Press, 1996), pp. 10–48.

[20] Letter from Colin Rowe to Nicholas and Victoria Boyarsky, May 6, 1991, ABA.

[21] For a discussion about Boyarsky's postcard collection, see Igor Marjanović, "Wish You Were Here: Alvin Boyarsky's Chicago Postcards," in Katerina Ruedi Ray and Charles Waldheim, eds., *Chicago Architecture: Histories, Revisions, Alternatives* (Chicago: University of Chicago Press, 2005), pp. 207–225.

[22] Alvin Boyarsky, "Camillo Sitte: City Builder," p. 97.

[23] Boyarsky's book title is mentioned in his short biography accompanying "Chicago *à la Carte*."

[24] Ibid., p. 600.

[25] Ibid., p. 595.

[26] Ibid., p. 631.

[27] A. T. Burch, "Marina Towers: One of Chicago's Living Art Forms," *Chicago Daily News* (September 5, 1964).

[28] Alvin Boyarsky, "Chicago *à la Carte*," p. 622.

[29] Ibid., pp. 638, 640.

[30] Alvin Boyarsky, "O'Hare: Air Pollution," unedited notes for "Chicago *à la Carte*," ABA.

[31] Alvin Boyarsky, "Chicago *à la Carte*," p. 636.

[32] Ibid., p. 637.

[33] Rem Koolhaas, "*Junkspace*" *October*, vol. 100 (Spring 2002), pp. 175–190.

[34] Rem Koolhaas, "Atlanta," in Robin Middleton, *Architectural Associations*, p. 85. Koolhaas describes his first encounter with Boyarsky, while he lectured on Chicago.

[35] Rem Koolhaas, *Delirious New York* (New York: Monacelli Press, 1994), p. 40. For a comparison between the use of postcards by Boyarsky and Koolhaas, see Igor Marjanović, "Postcards and the Making of Architectural History: The Cases of Alvin Boyarsky and Rem Koolhaas," in Robert Alexander Gonzalez and Marylis Rebeca Nepomechie, eds., *Archipelagos: Outposts of the Americas* (Washington, DC: ACSA Press, 2004), pp. 571–577.

[36] Alvin Boyarsky, "Chicago *à la Carte*," p. 612.

[37] Rem Koolhaas, *S, M, L, XL* (New York: The Monacelli Press, 1994), pp. 495–516.

[38] Grahame Shane wrote a detailed account of IID in his unpublished essay "The IID Summer Sessions, 1970–1972," circa 1992. See also Igor Marjanović, "Cheerful Chats: Alvin Boyarsky and the Art of Teaching Critical Architecture" in Renata Hejduk and Harry van Oudenallen, eds., *The Art of Architecture, The Science of Architecture* (Washington, DC: ACSA Press, 2005), pp. 186–194, and Irene Sunwoo, "Pedagogy's Progress: Alvin Boyarsky's International Institute of Design," *Grey Room*, 34 (Winter 2009), pp. 28–57.

[39] Alvin Boyarsky, "S.S. 71," *Architectural Design*, XLIII (April 1972), p. 220.

[40] Alvin Boyarsky, "Chicago *à la Carte*," p. 638.

[41] Alvin Boyarsky, "Summer Session 1971," *Architectural Design* (April 1972), p. 220. This phrasing was also used on the 1971 promotional postcards for the sessions that were held at the ABA.

[42] For a connection between IID and post-modernist discourses, see Graham Shane, "The IID Summer Sessions 1970-1972."

[43] Alvin Boyarsky, interview by Bill Mount, 1980, ABA.

[44] Ibid.

[45] Dennis Crompton, in conversation with the author, November 24, 2005.

[46] "Ambience and Alchemy: Alvin Boyarsky Interviewed," *Architectural Review* (October 1983), pp. 27–31.

[47] On the role of home, displacement, and collecting in Boyarsky's pedagogical model at the AA, see Igor Marjanović, "Alvin Boyarsky's Delicatessen," in Jane Rendell, Jonathan Hill, Murray Fraser, and Mark Dorrian, eds., *Critical Architecture* (London: Routledge, 2007), pp. 190–199. For other discussions on Boyarsky's AA tenure, see David Dunster, "Boyarsky and the Architectural Association," in Paul Davies and Torsten Schmiedeknecht, eds., *An Architect's Guide to Fame* (Oxford: Architectural Press, 2005), pp. 33–50, and Andrew Higgott, "Searching for the Subject: Alvin Boyarsky and the Architectural Association," in *Mediating Modernism: Architectural Cultures in Britain* (London: Routledge, 2006), pp. 154–177.

[48] Alvin Boyarsky, "The History of the AA," undated, ABA.

[49] Alvin Boyarsky, "The AA School and Projects," undated lecture transcript, ABA.

THE BIG GIZMO

BART LOOTSMA

Buckminster Fuller's Dymaxion House is as much about Chicago as Le Corbusier's Pavillon de l'Esprit Nouveau is about Paris. Le Corbusier's pavilion at the "Exposition internationale des arts décoratifs et industriels modernes" in 1925 was not just a prototype for a house. It also showed the *Plan Voisin* for Paris, which proposed to replace large parts of the city's center with large towers related to Saint-Simonist *industriels*. The flirt with *industriels* continued inside the pavilion with selected furniture and building elements that would be advertised in the magazine *Esprit Nouveau.*

In one of his lectures, Buckminster Fuller recounts how buyers from Chicago visited the 1925 "Exposition" in order to outdo the New York stores as *the* place to see the latest designs and products by the European avant-garde, from the Bauhaus to the Constructivists. To sell the modern furniture bought in Europe, the Marshall Field's Department Store used the Dymaxion House as a backdrop so futuristic that the furniture shown in it would look only modestly modern and the clientele were able to get used to it before the "Century of Progress" was to be ushered in at Chicago's World's Fair of 1933. The name "Dymaxion" was invented so that the audience would not mistake the strange biscuit tin for a Bauhaus design.

The Pavillon de L'Esprit Nouveau and the Dymaxion House were prototypes for machines to live in. Whereas Le Corbusier adapted urbanism, architecture, and design for the new *industriels* in an evolutionary process, Buckminster Fuller came with what Reyner Banham would call a *gizmo:* a patented and industrially produced device that seemed to come from nowhere but with which one could theoretically survive anywhere. The Dymaxion House was packed with as many gadgets and gimmicks as possible: an electro-vacuum oven, a refrigerator, a dishwasher, a television, a dicta-phone, and a gramophone. The American buyers must have understood and loved it immediately.

DYMAXION HOUSE AT MARSHALL FIELD'S DEPARTMENT STORE, BUCKMINSTER FULLER, 1929.

CHICAGO FRAME AS PICTURE FRAME

BARRY BERGDOLL

Twice in his career Mies van der Rohe proposed a fundamental change of our conception of the city through a paradigmatic tall building. The first, unbuilt, was in the early 1920s when he drew up an unforgettable image of a fully glazed skyscraper at Friedrichstrasse in response to the question if Berlin could follow the lead of Chicago and host a high-rise office building in its urban core. The second, as fate would have it, was in 1948 in Chicago, where he formulated a radical new aesthetic and ethic of the American skyscraper that gave form in a new way both to a Chicago city block, and to his own dream of two decades earlier. "Only skyscrapers under construction reveal their bold constructive thoughts," Mies wrote in 1922 and continued: "Then, the impression made by their soaring skeletal frames is overwhelming [...]. On the other hand, when the structure is later covered with masonry this impression is destroyed and the constructive character denied [...]." In the twin apartment towers at 860–880 Lake Shore Drive, Mies brought the columnar grid of the American steel-frame – theorized sixty years earlier by Louis Sullivan – outside the volumetric envelope, preserving space for a flexible plan and the beauty of the skeleton in construction in the final form. Textbooks have retained the breakthrough of Mies's newly textured façade, with its rich play of shadow and reflection. Yet a major innovation was in extending the notion of the structural frame from construction to experience. Obeying the demand by the landseller, Northwestern University, to preserve lake views, Mies structured the voids as well as the solids. The skel-

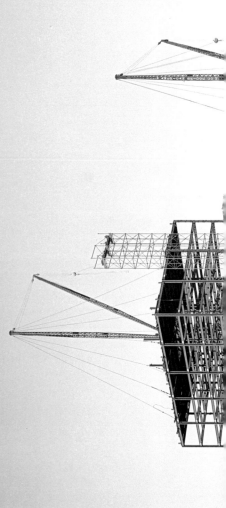

etal frame served as a picture frame, defining the horizon over the sublime expanse of Lake Michigan from under its one-story extrusion as a colonnade connecting the towers. In the apartments floor-to-ceiling glass presented a framed diorama view stretching to infinity.

860–880 LAKE SHORE DRIVE APARTMENTS, LUDWIG MIES VAN DER ROHE, 1951.

THE RATIONAL, INTERNATIONAL OCCULT

KONRAD WACHSMANN AND
THE EXPERIMENTAL DIGITIZATION OF ARCHITECTURE

JOHN HARWOOD

When Konrad Wachsmann disembarked in New York Harbor in 1941 – after eight years fleeing the Nazi regime through Italy, Spain, and France – he arrived not as an architect but as an "intellectual."[1] A Jewish lawyer, Jerome Hard, Wachsmann's former client Albert Einstein, a New York stockbroker named Charles Allen, the art historian Richard Krautheimer, and Walter Gropius had all written to the American consulate in Marseille to certify that Wachsmann's technological expertise and fame as the author of *Holzhausbau* qualified him for an "intellectual visa" to emigrate to the United States. He soon abandoned any effort to establish himself in a conventional architectural practice, instead devoting himself to "analytical studies of research and development in industrialization, including standardization, modular coordination, mechanical integration, economics, production technology, development of processes, tools, machines and methods of assembly."[2] By 1967, Wachsmann owned over one hundred individual patents in numerous countries, yet he had designed only a small handful of buildings.[3]

Wachsmann's immediate trajectory led him to Harvard University, where he worked on experimental projects for the US military, collaborating with Erich Mendelsohn and Antonin Raymond on the "typical German and Japanese test structures" that were to be bombed at Dugway Proving Ground in Utah in preparation for the massive aerial bombardment of the Axis powers in 1944 and 1945.[4] In 1946, Wachsmann and Gropius also famously formed the legendary late failure of the modernist dream of mass-produced housing, the General Panel Corporation (GPC).[5] That project took him to Burbank, California, and in the immediate post-World War II period he traveled widely in the US and Europe in conjunction with an exhibition on his work sponsored by the Museum of Modern Art and the United States Information Agency (USIA).[6]

AN UNEASY WELCOME TO CHICAGO

By 1951, the GPC was bankrupt, but the scheme and the funding his military projects brought in had earned Wachsmann a reputation as a leading expert in mass-production and space frame technology, resulting in an invitation to join the faculty at Mies van der Rohe's architecture school at the Illinois Institute of Technology (IIT) in Chicago. Here, he would head up the Department of Advanced Building Research, located not on the school's new campus but in a satellite building on the Near North Side, held jointly by IIT and László Moholy-Nagy's Institute of Design, which was then under the directorship of Serge Chermayeff and later, Crombie Taylor (1951–1955) and Jay Doblin (1955–1969).[7]

This department was an effort on the part of IIT to secure, like many other architecture schools during the period, funding from the federal government and industry that was aimed at securing a smooth transition from the wartime economy to peacetime by adapting newly invented and manufactured war material to useful ends in the construction industry.[8] Wachsmann's expertise in construction was therefore the basis of his newfound position; however, he stretched beyond his brief when he discovered the "wonderful [...] world of research and teaching" in the numerous institutions of higher education in Chicago.[9]

Despite the mutual influence Wachsmann and Mies had upon one another, especially in terms of their interest in exploiting steel space frames to create massive clear-span interiors (what Wachsmann and Mies alike referred to as "Ultimate Space"), it is plain that Wachsmann's thought and teaching were at odds with the poetic basis of Mies's curriculum.[10] In fact, Wachsmann's relationship with Mies was constantly strained, even at its best moments. As Wachsmann recalled in an unpublished memoir on the various members of the faculty at the Bauhaus, Mies was irrevocably nostalgic and even sinister in his staunch opposition to the epistemological shifts engendered by post-World War II weapons and information technology: "I saw him as Schinkel's disciple [...] Now, as then, he appears to me with a magic stigma of a pentagram on his chest like a reawakened Golem."[11]

64 KONRAD WACHSMANN, DESIGN FOR AIRPLANE HANGAR FOR THE UNITED STATES ARMY AIR FORCE, 1950–1951.

A "CHICAGO SCHOOL" OF CYBERNETICS

The cause of this tension was that, by the turn of the 1950s, the failure of the GPC had pushed Wachsmann to entertain a new intellectual commitment to the emerging syncretic science of cybernetics. The heady ideas of a circle of scientists, engineers, and philosophers then beginning to gather at the University of Illinois at Urbana-Champaign and the University of Chicago appear to have marked him deeply–figures such as the path-breaking computer researcher Gerald S. Blum, the automata theoretician Heinz von Foerster, and the English psychiatrist W. Ross Ashby after 1960. Perhaps closest to his heart was the "anti-" or "trans-Aristotelian" German emigré philosopher, engineer, and professor at UIUC Gotthard Günther, whom Wachsmann quoted epigraphically to frame his own publications and teaching. As Günther summarized his work since the 1930s, aimed at supplanting traditional binary logical systems (e.g. Aristotelian and Boolean logic) with "many-valued systems," in 1962:

Since it is impossible to deny the existence of novel methods and positive results produced by cybernetic research, we have no choice but to develop a new system of ontology together with a corresponding theory of logic. The logical methods that are used faute de mieux in cybernetics belong to the old ontological tradition and are not powerful enough to analyze the fresh aspects of Reality that are beginning to emerge from a theory of automata [...]. It is not possible to develop a new ontological theory of logic by starting at the bottom. Aristotle did not do so.[12]

Although it is unlikely that Wachsmann fully digested either the mathematics or the complex philosophical logic that characterizes Günther's unusual work, he was able to find in it not only a justification of the failure of the GPC, but also a conceptual blueprint for his future work–a top-down reformation of the theory of architecture. He realized that by beginning with the factory, rather than with the systematic reorganization of architecture within an institutional and analytical structure, his project had always been doomed to failure. Günther's "morphogrammatical" alternative logical systems offered Wachsmann compelling evidence that a new set of assumptions, based upon three- and four-dimensional logics, could overcome economic, social, and technical obstacles to the industrialization and automation of building.

Wachsmann seems to have found Günther's experiments in formal logic compelling as models for architectural form and design processes as well. Günther's multivalent morphogrammatics were essays in iterative substitution, supplanting one element within a set with another, and thus impacting the quality and quantity of the set as a whole. The dense web of interrelationships between elements–laid out in diagrams accompanying Günther's texts as a network of interconnected boxes–must have appeared to Wachsmann as isomorphs of the joining elements in his space frames. Such isomorphisms also help to explain Wachsmann's most unusual and lasting design from his years at IIT, an intricate space frame system of wishbone-shaped elements in which none of the rigid structural members touch at the joints. This structural idea, of a system in pure tension, has since become an icon of the intersection between architecture and network theory.[13]

Although he was estranged from the day-to-day goings-on in Crown Hall, sequestered in a building off of the main campus, Wachsmann soon gathered around him a group of students who were eager to work with him on solving the problems of mass-production in modern architecture and establishing a firmer logical basis for

65

architectural design. Intended as a complement to the teachings and planning projects of Ludwig Hilberseimer, who had headed the urban planning program at IIT since his arrival from Germany in 1938 (when it was still Armour Institute of Technology) and who eventually went on to direct Chicago's city planning office, Wachsmann's building research curriculum aimed at adapting mass-production and collaborative design techniques to ease the completion of the numerous public and private housing projects then springing up across the city during the post-war building boom. Yet Wachsmann used this imperative to expand the purview of his program well beyond housing. Spurred by a commission from the Federal Housing Agency for further research into mass-produced housing, in the autumn of 1951 Wachsmann became perhaps the first architect to apply computer science, in the form of programs written and processed on punch cards, to architectural design.

Wachsmann's method was unusual to say the least, and clearly not entirely derived from computer science or from the mechanical requirements of the punch

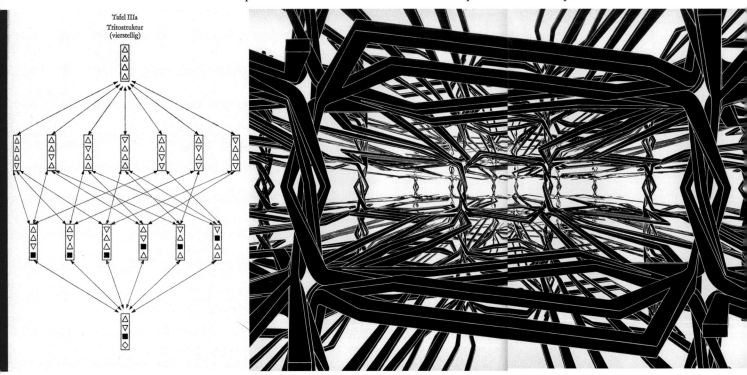

LEFT: GOTTHARD GÜNTHER, MORPHOGRAMMATICAL SYSTEM ("TRIOSTRUKTUR"), 1967.
RIGHT: KONRAD WACHSMANN, SPACE FRAME, 1953. DETAIL VIEW.

card apparatus, neither of which he appears to have wholly grasped. The theoretical impulse was the same as that underlying the later effort to develop "design methods"; Wachsmann reasoned that "an information machine" could help to manage the complexity of "environmental" and "structural" constraints, and provide ready-made rational decisions for the designer.[14]

The ambitious primary aim of the project was to identify the determinant causes–the underlying forces, be they material, economic, social, etc.–of architecture, and to re-theorize design practice as the technical restructuring of the process of design itself. As he commented in a presentation of the results of the project in *Bauen und Wohnen* after nearly a decade of work (the same article in which he cited Günther's cybernetic philosophy),

it is the way of going about things that conditions the success of any enterprise. Industry and the new laws of energy condition the life and structure of our epoch. Thus, electricity, in so far as it produces light, influences, determines, and alters the human conception of darkness. The same thing cannot be said for electric lights. The cause is electric energy and not the light itself. Similarly in the case of architecture, cause precedes effect.[15]

If architecture was to be adapted to industrialization, it would have to make architectural the organizational logic of industry. To this end, Wachsmann and his students

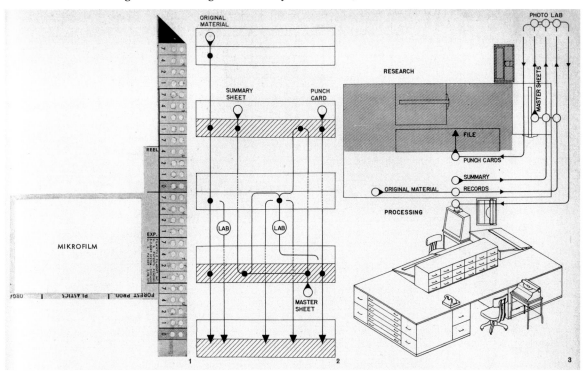

67 KONRAD WACHSMANN AND IIT STUDENTS, MODULAR COORDINATION CLASSFICATION SYSTEM, 1951–1952. SCHEMATIC DIAGRAM AND VIEW OF STUDIO APPARATUS.

designed a "trial modular-coordinate classification" system, integrating a punch card sorter, microfilm, filing cabinets, projectors, and drafting tables into an apparatus that would continually catalogue an ever-growing database of information on architectural production. As Wachsmann summarized the design in 1959:

The principle of this system consists in registering no matter what datum-information, texts, designs, symbols, and others-on microfilm. The data from these films are then punched on appropriate cards. These cards allow for all the combinations of information desired. Moreover, it is possible to place the punched card in a projector-this being combined with microfilm-so as to study the figure shown on the film. It is possible, obviously, to photocopy this figure.[16]

Regardless of the awkwardness of this early scheme for computerizing architecture, which on the surface appears to have been little more than making shadow puppets with punch cards and dreaming of utopian institutions, Wachsmann was at pains to create a means for rationally and mechanically expanding the purview of the designer. These apparatuses, for which he produced a design in plan and isometric, were intended to become "standard equipment for technical training colleges, research institutes, libraries, firms, public and private organizations, etc."[17] The cards were of Wachsmann's own design (patented and copyrighted by him for IIT in 1951), and

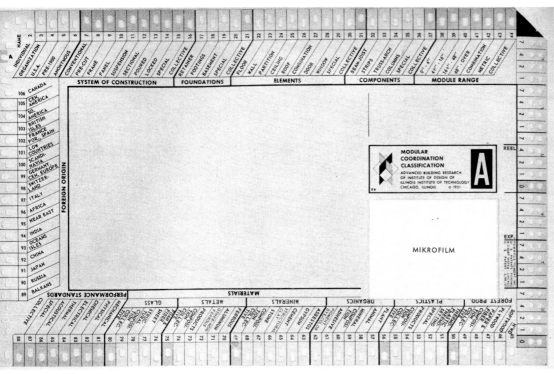

68   KONRAD WACHSMANN AND IIT STUDENTS, MODULAR COORDINATION CLASSIFICATION PUNCH CARD [VERSION A], 1951–1952.

aimed to document the totality of a building's becoming. Drawing, so long thought to hold the key to understanding the logic of architectural design (and certainly a center-piece of Mies's curriculum at IIT), would become only one part of a broader represen-tational apparatus, reducible to a datum within an organizational diagram.

As he acknowledged in an introductory caveat, this punch card was not easy to read: "It is vital to stress that the results achieved by a team are often secondary. Success is not always apparent. The value of the work is often methodological in nature."[18] Yet there was hope for it as a new mode of design, provided that the system was taken up as part of a holistic reform of higher education in architecture and beyond: "The results of study and analysis [will be] registered and then become part of the program of schools and universities. An international center is to be charged with the organization of this vast form of teamwork."[19] In Wachsmann's ambitious vision, the Bauhaus ideal of collaboration had been transformed into a trans-national cybernetic system of governance, loosely modeled upon the university-based collaborative research institutions he had discovered in Chicago–a "research institute," comprising specialists working in "basic research, material research, production technology, modular coordination, statics, product research, environmental control, installations, hygiene, organization, statistics, sociology, psychology, planning."[20] In this sense, he shared the broad ambitions of his fellow Bauhaus émigrés to Chicago–such as László Moholy-Nagy and Ludwig Hilberseimer–to redefine the Bauhaus project; yet his own vision departed from theirs in the sense that he aimed to accomplish pedagogical, technical, and conceptual reforms in architectural culture through the collaborative efforts in the sciences given new license through the culture of applied cybernetics.[21] As he put it in his posthumously published memoir, due to the possibilities of collaboration "between the Institute of Design and the Institute of Technology, I could access almost unlimited areas of expertise."[22] That expertise was not only in the experimental aesthetics of Moholy-Nagy and György Kepes, or the regional planning techniques of Hilberseimer, but in natural and applied science departments in Chicago and the surrounding area.

WACHSMANN FROM CHICAGO TO THE WORLD

Despite its shortcomings, obvious in hindsight, his trans-national, computer-based approach to architectural research seems to have had a broad appeal, and it was productive of an immense body of architectural and engineering work. He left Chicago behind during winters and summers, traveling abroad to showcase his para-cybernetic research. In 1954, Wachsmann returned to Germany as a guest lecturer at Egon Eiermann's chair at the Technische Hochschule in Karlsruhe; two years later he lectured at the Hochschule für Technik in Stuttgart. In winter 1955, perhaps due to connections garnered during his earlier collaboration with Antonin Raymond on the Dugway project, he led a research seminar at the University of Tokyo. In the summers of

1956, 1957, and 1958, he led "Teamarbeit" at the International Summer Academy in Salzburg, and also stopped by the AA in London to lecture on automation and feedback at the invitation of Peter Smithson. And in the summer of 1959, he led a similar project at the École Polytechnique in Lausanne. Meanwhile, over the period between 1954 and 1959, USIA-sponsored exhibits of Wachsmann's work, called *Bauen in unserer Zeit* (Building in Our Time), went on display in Vienna, Munich, Zurich, Rome, Amsterdam, Delft, and Essen, all of which were accompanied by Wachsmann's personal visits, to deliver a lectue with the same title.[23]

All of this work, plus Wachsmann's ongoing photographic practice,[24] formed the intellectual, technical, and graphic basis of his best-known work, the treatise *Wendepunkt im Bauen* (*The Turning Point of Building*), published in German in 1959 and translated into French, English, Italian, and Japanese shortly thereafter. As he noted with pride in his preface, the publisher–Krausskopf–was not an architectural publisher but mainly a technology-oriented press, "primarily concerned with industrial and technological topics such as the flow of materials, automation, regulatory and control systems, [and] hydraulics."[25]

The reformulation of the history of modern architecture in *Wendepunkt* is well-known, orienting the contrast between *Architektur* and *Baukunst* around purely techno-spatial concerns rather than typical art-historical and architectural theoretical concerns regarding the interrelations between *parti*, ornament, and structure. And certainly Wachsmann's obsession with the universal joint, present in his work since World War II, is the primary object of investigation.[26] Less well remembered, however, is the

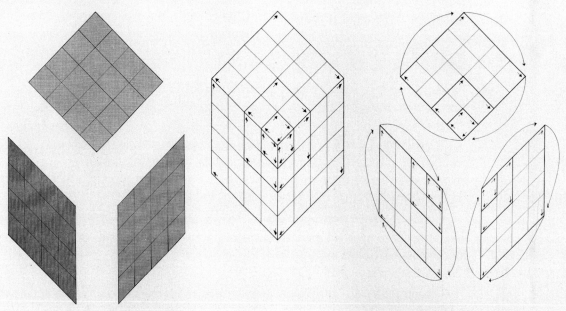

69 The separation of the faces of the cube into three distinct but interdependent planes
70 The dynamic relationships of the individual parts of an arbitrarily subdivided cube

71 The separated planes of the cube, in which dimensions and movement are simultaneously determined, express time as an additional, indispensable factor in establishing measurements

70   KONRAD WACHSMANN, DIAGRAMS OF "PLANE RASTERS ISSUING ON THREE SIDES FROM THE INNER CENTER OF AN IMAGINARY CUBE," IN *WENDEPUNKT IM BAUEN*, 1959.

argument, running throughout, that the means for accomplishing this "dissolution of architectonic contours" and "elastically" adapting the architectural enclosure to its program was *not* the joint itself but its means of production. Wachsmann placed emphasis on two strategies: First, the reformulation of the joint as nothing more than a material register of a spatio-temporal field of energies figured by the three-dimensional Cartesian grid, or raster, which would be envisaged and controlled by a computer; and second, the *automatic control* of machines that would produce these fields in lieu of architecture.[27] (In this last case, the archetype of this process is the mechanical jig, or universal machine for moving building materials in space and controlling other power tools that work on the materials.)

The success of *Wendepunkt* meant increased freedom for Wachsmann to pursue this project, and he soon decamped from IIT for the University of Southern California, where he became the first chair of its new Building Institute. Although he had found the city of Chicago a fertile ground for experimentation, Wachsmann believed that in Los Angeles he would be free from the overwhelming influence of Mies. From this position he attempted (and spectacularly failed to achieve) the redesign of the entire university.[28] The central node of this project was to be Wachsmann himself, or rather a book-entitled *Between Space and Time*-that aimed to offer a complete description of the entire universe intertwined with Wachsmann's autobiography, to be exactly 500 pages long. This would be connected to several other multimedia projects, including a "prime time" television program, a film series, radio broadcasts, newspaper columns, and an ever-expanding series of diagrams-derived from the raster systems he designed throughout the 1950s-that would represent in "real time" the unfolding of a perfect rational system of intercoordinated specialists. In short, through his engagement with cybernetics, Wachsmann became paranoid, a mystic. He re-theorized and embodied the architect as a *medium*-a means of holding together diffuse cultural and productive

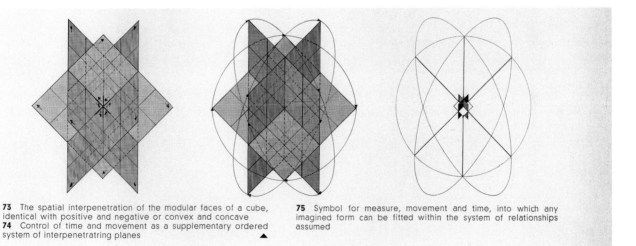

73 The spatial interpenetration of the modular faces of a cube, identical with positive and negative or convex and concave
74 Control of time and movement as a supplementary ordered system of interpenetratring planes ▲

75 Symbol for measure, movement and time, into which any imagined form can be fitted within the system of relationships assumed

71   KONRAD WACHSMANN, SPATIAL INTERPRETATION OF THE MODULAR CUBE IN RELATION TO TIME AND MOVEMENT, IN *WENDEPUNKT IM BAUEN*, 1959.

activities, making them visible to one another, and engendering multiple feedback loops between independent processes.

The central figure and structure of this new mode of organizing all human knowledge was the figure of the raster and universal joint, now transformed into a fractal-like armature, which also reproduceed the magical symbol of two interlocked triangles, or the Star of David, emphasizing the mystical properties of the number seven and Wachsmann's Jewish heritage. Each component of Wachsmann's massive imaginary organization takes on the same form—for instance, within the "Building Research Division" of the organization, the "Information Center Library," "Teacher Training," "Research Testing," "Faculty," "Graduate Studies," and "Educational Studies" all have the same heptavalent form, further subdivided into categories, artefacts, or activities. Such radically different terms as "coordination," "maps and plans," "faculty council," "methodology," "biological responses," "individual," and "market"—to take but seven random examples—are made into equivalencies. Through this structure, Wachsmann argued, USC would create "the cadre of trained research experts who, based on comprehensive, international information-retrieval, and in closest collaboration under the assumed new academic order [...] shall become the creative analysts and designers for the rational and the emotional cycle of the society of man."[29]

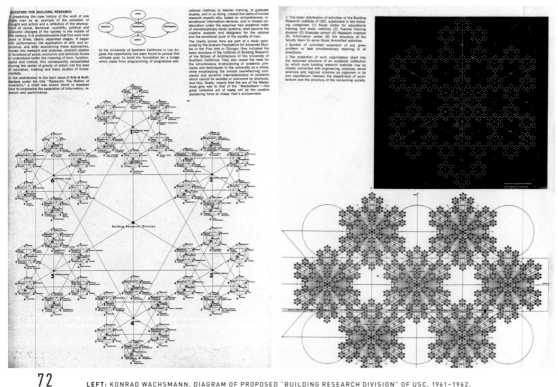

72   LEFT: KONRAD WACHSMANN, DIAGRAM OF PROPOSED "BUILDING RESEARCH DIVISION" OF USC, 1961–1962.
       RIGHT: KONRAD WACHSMANN, DIAGRAM OF PROPOSED REORGANIZATION OF USC, 1961–1962.

Despite the apparent insanity of this project—its occultism, or operating in secret—it does not take much historical work or critical thought to connect the metaphysical assumptions undergirding Wachsmann's obsessions to many contemporary efforts to automate architectural production, expand architectural theory to cover other spheres of cultural endeavor, or to re-envision architecture as one "system" or another.

This essay is based upon part of the research I originally conducted in preparation for the conference "Return Emigrations" at Columbia University in January 2009; I would like to thank the conference organizers, Richard Anderson and Lynette Widder, and the conference participants for their helpful comments. I later presented additional research on a similar topic for the panel "Chicago in the World" at the Society of Architectural Historians Annual Meeting in 2010; my thanks to Alexander Eisenschmidt and Jonathan Mekinda for the invitation to share my work there and in this volume.

[1] Wachsmann's narrow escape from the concentration camps of the Axis powers and occupied France are related in Michael Grüning, *Der Wachsmann-Report: Auskünfte eines Architekten* (Basel, Boston, and Berlin: Birkhäuser, 2001). Since this account is based upon Wachsmann's own rather late and occasionally unreliable recollections, recounted in an informal interview transcript format, I have tried to check his accounts against various documents of earlier date, e.g. his curricula vitae from the Konrad Wachsmann Archive (KWA) (AK88). Copies of affidavits filed on Wachsmann's behalf with the American consulate in Marseille by Krautheimer and Gropius, testifying to his technological expertise, are preserved in the KWA (AK88). The claim for Wachsmann's intellectual status was reinforced throughout the 1950s, '60s, and '70s; see, for example, Carlo Testa, *The Industrialization of Building* (New York, etc.: Van Nostrand Reinhold Company, 1972), especially chapter 8 on "the future of industrialized building" and "the need for a controlling authority," which declares Wachsmann's writings as authoritative and world-historical.

[2] Quoted in the special issue on Wachsmann's work, *Arts & Architecture,* 84 (May 1967), pp. 6–27, here p. 12.

[3] Wachsmann's US Patents (nos. 2, 355,192; 2,421,305; 2,426,802; 2,491,882; 2,599,741; 3,065,831; and 3,175,657) are available on-line through Google Patent Search and the US Patent and Trademark Office, www.uspto.org.

[4] On the Dugway experiments, see Enrique Ramirez, "Built to Destroy: Erich Mendelsohn's, Konrad Wachsmann's 'Typical German and Japanese Test Structures' at Dugway Proving Ground, Utah," Master's Thesis, Yale University, 2007.

[5] On the General Panel Corporation, see Gilbert Herbert, *The Dream of the Factory-Made House: Walter Gropius and Konrad Wachsmann* (Cambridge, MA: MIT Press, 1984); Herman Herrey, "At last we have a prefabrication system which enables architects to design any type of building with three-dimensional modules," *The New Pencil Points* (April 1943), pp. 36–47; and Adolf Stiller, "The House as an Article on the Way to Production," *A+T*, 10 (1997), pp. 34–47, which places Gropius and Wachsmann's work in a broader context of international efforts to create mass-produced housing.

[6] Images of these exhibits are reproduced in *Arts and Architecture,* 84 (May 1967), pp. 6–27.

[7] In Taylor and Doblin, Wachsmann found staunch allies; both were firmly committed to the application of communications and information theory to architecture and industrial design. Taylor invited Wachsmann to join him at USC when he became Associate Dean of Architecture there in 1962, appointing Wachsmann to the directorship of the newly founded Building Institute (discussed below). On Taylor, see K. Flynn, "Crombie Taylor–Architect," *http://www.tanglenet.com/taylor_bio.htm* (accessed December 24, 2012). On Doblin, see his essay "Mass Media: The Stimulation System," *Dot Zero*, 3 (Spring 1967).

[8] On this broad-based effort to pursue "research" into construction in North American architecture schools, see Joan Ockman, ed., *Architecture School: Three Centuries of Educating Architects in North America* (Cambridge, MA: MIT Press, 2012); and Avigail Sachs, "Research for Architecture: Building a Discipline and Modernizing the Profession" (Ph.D. Dissertation, University of California at Berkeley, 2009).

[9] Grüning, *Der Wachsmann-Report*, p. 532.

[10] On the architecture curriculum at IIT, see Rolf Achilles, Keven Harrington and Charlotte Myhrum, eds., *Mies van der Rohe, Architect as Educator* (Chicago: Mies van der Rohe Centennial Project, Illinois Institute of Technology, University of Chicago Press, 1986).

[11] Konrad Wachsmann, unpublished manuscript for introduction to Howard Dearstyne, *Inside the Bauhaus* (Los Angeles: Hennessey and Ingalls, 1975), pp. 13–14, KWA AK85.

[12] Gotthard Günther, "Cybernetic Ontology and Transjunctional Operations," in Marshall C. Yovits, George T. Jacobi and Gordon D. Goldstein, eds., *Self-Organizing Systems* (Washington, DC: Spartan Books, 1962), pp. 313–392, 313, 316.

[13] A quick Google search for images of Wachsmann's space frame yields hundreds of hits, as many from blogs devoted to architecture as to information sciences. See also Mark Wigley, "Network Fever," *Grey Room*, 4 (Summer 2001), pp. 82–122, for which Wachsmann's design serves as the frontispiece.

[14] Konrad Wachsmann, "Studium im Team," *Bauen und Wohnen*, 14 (October 1960), pp. 350–384. On design methods, see Alise Upitis, "Nature Normative: the Design Methods Movement, 1944–1967" (Ph.D. Dissertation, Massachussetts Institute of Technology, 2008).

[15] Wachsmann, "Studium im Team," p. 350.

[16] Ibid., p. 350.

[17] Ibid., p. 357.

[18] Ibid., p. 350.

[19] Ibid., p. 350.

[20] Konrad Wachsmann, *The Turning Point in Building: Structure and Design*, trans. Thomas E. Burton (New York: Reinhold, 1961), p. 229.

[21] On Moholy-Nagy's "New Bauhaus" in Chicago and its subsequent influence on American architectural culture, see Reinhold Martin, *The Organizational Complex: Architecture, Media, and Corporate Space* (Cambridge, MA: MIT Press, 2003), chapter 2. On the "inter-" or "multidisciplinary" nature of cybernetic culture, see Orit N. Halpern, *Beautiful Data: A History of Vision and Reason since 1945* (Durham, NC: Duke University Press, 2013).

[22] Grüning, *Der Wachsmann-Report*, p. 543.

[23] The full text of the lecture, delivered 28 February 1957, and commentary by Peter Smithson after the lecture is reprinted in Konrad Wachsmann, "Building in Our Time," *AA Journal*, 72 (April 1957), pp. 224-233, 225.

[24] On the relationship of Wachsmann's photography to his cybernetic thought, see his book of photographs *Aspekte* (Wiesbaden: Krausskopf, 1961). Interestingly, the introductory text (unpaginated) to his collection of photographs of classical and Renaissance monuments and vernacular architecture of Italian hill towns borrows liberally from the information theorist Abraham Moles: "Die Welt, von der wir zurückblicken, ist eine andere. Es ist eine ganz neue Epoche, bedingt durch den Triumph der wissenschaftlichen Erkenntnisse, der elektrischen Energie [...]. Das nukleare Zeitalter eröffnete den Weltraum, und was der Mensch dort erblickt, muss er in die Sprache irdischen Verstehens übersetzen, so wie es die Zeit ihm erlaubt." Compare to A. Moles in *Epoche Atom und Automation: Enzyklopädie des technischen Jahrhunderts* (Frankfurt am Main: Wilhelm-Limpert-Verlag, 1958), chapter "Einführung."

[25] Wachsmann, *The Turning Point of Building*, preface.

[26] On Wachsmann's preoccupation with joints, see Kenneth Frampton, "I tecnocrati della Pax Americana: Wachsmann & Fuller," *Casabella*, 52, no. 542/543 (January/February 1988), pp. 40–45.

[27] See Wachsmann, *The Turning Point of Building*, pp. 50–51, 103.

[28] Wachsmann was a nearly permanent thorn in the side of the administration at USC, writing memorandum after memorandum to the president and academic officers regarding what he saw as necessary reforms to the institution, most of which involved allowing Wachsmann himself to redesign the curriculum of the whole university entirely on his own. Needless to say, none of these changes were implemented, and the interdisciplinary seminars that Wachsmann held at USC became little more than a minor countercultural clique isolated in the architecture school. Documents pertaining to Wachsmann's late, paranoid project are preserved in the KWA: Konrad Wachsmann, "Excerpts of the Introduction to the Manuscript with the Working Title 'Between Time and Space' by Konrad Wachsmann," 1977, KWA AK87; Konrad Wachsmann, "A preliminary, unedited, first draft of a Synopsis for a one-hour T.V. Cassette Film with the working title: 'Science and Technology' as part of a presently proposed 22 program T.V. Cassette series with the working title: 'Symposium' or 'Novus Ordo Seclorum,'" KWA AK 87/2; and lecture titles and notes from KWA AK88.

[29] Wachsmann, quoted in *Arts & Architecture*, 84 (May 1967), pp. 6–30, p. 28.

AUTOMATIC URBANISM

ALEXANDER EISENSCHMIDT

The geographic center of Chicago is the site of a truly superlative urban spectacle – a surrealist experiment under the guise of infrastructure. What Daniel H. Burnham had previously envisioned as a cultural Civic Center for his *Plan of Chicago* is today the Circle Interchange – an infrastructural mammoth formed by the intersection of the Congress Parkway, three expressways (Dan Ryan, Eisenhower, and Kennedy), and pierced by the city's Blue line train that transitions here from surface operation to subway. The hybrid states of mobility are set square into the city. Three hundred thousand vehicles converge daily and take part in a collective event, a manifestation of the distortions of time and space. While the interchange is a product of rational engineering and purposeful machining, solely driven by ambitions to smooth out the discontinuities between different flows of traffic, it is everyday witness to some of the city's slowest vehicular travel, estimated at a combined loss of twenty-five million hours per year. As the logistics of velocity (or in our case slowness) govern each turn, the on-and-off routes, sweeping ramps, and converging lanes carve inaccessible islands into the city. Zones that are conditioned and simultaneously held at bay by the "civilized" urbanism of the city around it and by the "advanced" urbanism of infrastructure within it, result here in alternative zones that evade definition. The urbanism that the Circle Interchange thrusts into form not only abbreviates artistic gestures but, more importantly, amplifies spatial, programmatic, and atmospheric complexities. As the interchange systematically uproots and reverses its initial premises, we approximate a space that André Breton outlines as one where "the real and the imaginary, the past and the future, the communicable and the incommunicable, high and low, cease to be perceived as contradictions." This spatial concoction might be Chicago's most powerful *non sequitur*.

STACKED SUBURBIA

DAVID J. LEWIS

Designed by Bertrand Goldberg in 1959, and completed in 1967, Marina City sought to undo the precise urban concept that Chicago as a city had perfected, namely the separation of work and home. Marina City is the result of an excess of logic, the culmination of importing the amenities of the suburbs back into the heart of the city. But where the suburbs stretch horizontally, Marina City is stacked suburbia, complete with a leisure shopping mall, theater, restaurants, bowling alley, ice rink, yacht club, office park with conference facilities, parking promenade and modern, electrified leisure units with panoramic picture windows to the new urban pastoral. Commissioned by the Building Service Employees International Union, Marina City served as model of dense urban living that was paradoxically completely foreign in the temporally segregated, daily march of the business life that built Chicago's Loop. In its celebrated corn-cob shape, organized around an unprecedented central concrete core, Goldberg's invention placed on ceremonial public display, with no hint of irony, the very device that threatened the stability of his client's urban workplaces. Automobiles, now caught and captured for all remaining urbanites to see and judge, stare out at the city in all direction: a teenager's parking vista set on steroids, make-out point in the round.

MARINA CITY, BERTRAND GOLDBERG, 1967.

BANHAM'S MIESES

MARK LINDER

The story is legend, and perhaps even true: Alison and Peter Smithson's initial, brash, and tenacious declaration of their ambition to rehabilitate modern architecture in the wake of World War II arrived in Britain via Chicago in the form of a New Brutalist Mies. Acquainted with Ludwig Mies van der Rohe's new Chicago work only through recently published photographs and drawings in *Architects' Journal* and Philip Johnson's catalogue of the Museum of Modern Art's *Mies van der Rohe* exhibition,[1] the Smithsons' winning competition entry of 1949 for the Hunstanton Secondary Modern School emulated the surprising clarity, directness, and raw materiality of the steel, glass, and brick buildings Mies designed for the Illinois Institute of Technology. Mies's new idiom marked a departure from the luxurious surfaces and sleek styling of the two projects that had been most widely published in Britain before and after the war – the Barcelona Pavilion and the Tugendhat House[2] – and in it the Smithsons found the means to assert a stable, frank, and open architecture in a time of conflicted values and high stakes.[3] The Smithsons viewed Mies through the lens of post-war recovery

81   **LEFT:** MINERALS AND METALS RESEARCH BUILDING AT IIT, LUDWIG MIES VAN DER ROHE, *ARCHITECTS' JOURNAL*, JANUARY 1946.
RIGHT: HUNSTANTON SECONDARY MODERN SCHOOL, ALISON AND PETER SMITHSON, NORFOLK, ENGLAND, 1954, IN CHARLES JENCKS, *MODERN MOVEMENTS IN ARCHITECTURE*, 1971.

and efforts to revive the culture and economy of victorious but depleted Britain.[4] The shock of war and the urgency of rebuilding in its aftermath had unleashed debates about British identity and Britain's new role and engagement in international culture. The Smithsons contentiously inserted themselves into those debates at a key moment in the acceptance of modernism in Britain: with the exception of the policy of *The Architect and Building News* beginning in the late 1920s to feature examples of European modernism, and the publication in *Architectural Review* of projects by

Le Corbusier on the occasion of the English translation of *Vers une architecture* in 1927 (contrary to that journal's traditionalist stance at the time), it was not until the latter half of the 1930s that modern architecture began to have numerous advocates in practice or in the press, and not until the late 1940s that modernism began to flourish in the arts.[5]

The Smithsons' youthful embrace of Mies was the first of their many, varied, dogged, and contrarian attempts to redefine the ethos and modes of modernism that they would pursue in their subsequent work and which they and others would promote as the New Brutalism. Like many younger British architects, the Smithsons' aim was to creatively continue the experimentation and vision of pre-war work on the continent while evading its heroic and utopian claims. Their choice of Mies and adaption of his Chicago approach to conditions in Britain also might be understood as their first instance of engaging what they called the "as found" as well as an early demonstration of their canny ability to work with concepts or idioms that others also found interesting,

LEFT: WALTER SEGAL, OVINGTON SQUARE APARTMENT BLOCK, 1955.
RIGHT: PAGE FROM REYNER BANHAM, "THE NEW BRUTALISM," *ARCHITECTURAL REVIEW*, DECEMBER 1955.

but to do so while declaring a fundamentally different purpose or meaning. With Hunstanton, their first building, engaging Mies allowed them to acknowledge but swerve from post-war intellectual trends such as the neo-Palladian enthusiasms that followed Rudolph Wittkower's analyses of symbolic form and Colin Rowe's neo-classical formal analogies, or the modernist verities of functionalism, technical innovation, and social efficacy, or J. M. Richards's insistence on allying modernism with typically British cultural values, or Nikolas Pevsner's promotion of the picturesque and Englishness.

The Smithsons' New Brutalism would take other forms and find other sources over the next two decades, but they were joined by others in the early 1950s who also saw potential in Mies's new work. As Stephen Kite has noted, Colin St. John Wilson's Coventry Cathedral competition entry (1950–1951) was inspired by the space-frame airplane hangars of Konrad Wachsmann that later would be the basis for Mies's Chicago Convention Hall project (1954), and Wilson and others at the London County Council Architect's Department designed the housing estate at Albert Drive (1950–1952) to simulate the steel structure of the buildings at IIT through a combination of painted concrete slab edges and black brick cladding.[6] Another more ingenious, and even original, emulation of the Chicago Mies is Walter Segal's façade at Ovington Square (1955), which superimposes a light wooden grid supporting and containing the window units, painted black and easily mistaken for steel, in front of the two-tone brick cladding,

83 HUNSTANTON SECONDARY MODERN SCHOOL BY ALISON AND PETER SMITHSON IN REYNER BANHAM, "THE NEW BRUTALISM,"
ARCHITECTURAL REVIEW, DECEMBER 1955.

creating a complex geometric pattern of frames, voids, and glass and brick surfaces as well as a sense of lightness in an otherwise conventionally constructed apartment block.

LESS MIES

Yet, despite Mies's distinct role in the emergence of New Brutalism, his influence on the course of modern architecture in post-war Britain was hardly pervasive. Mies practically went missing from its development and assessment over the next decade, even from Reyner Banham's brilliant first attempt to define the principles of New Brutalism in his famous article of 1955, which had no images of work by Mies.[7] Even Hunstanton, the singular Miesian New Brutalist project, appeared only as a small image buried among others. Banham's clear intent to dissociate Mies and New Brutalism is evident in the only two references to Mies in the essay. The first is a curt estimation of Mies's significance for the Smithsons as nothing more than "one of the few recent examples of conceptual, form-giving design to which a young architect could turn at the time of its [Hunstanton's] conception."[8] The second occurs near the end of the article after Banham had made his case for New Brutalism as an architecture that coheres as "an image."[9] Banham insists (and protests too much) that "Miesian or Wittkowerian geometry was only an *ad hoc* device for the realization of 'Images'," and he doubles down by suggesting that "formality was discarded" after the photographic exhibition *Parallel of Art and Life* (1953), staged by the Smithsons and the artists Eduardo Paolozzi and Nigel Henderson at the Institute of Contemporary Arts (ICA) in London, because that show "enabled Brutalists to define their relationship to the visual world in terms of something other than geometry."[10]

Between those two mentions of Mies, which both cast him in strictly formal terms (even though the materialist, technical, and imagistic terms with which Banham defines New Brutalism could easily apply to Mies), there lies a huge difference, not between two understandings of Mies, but across a fundamental shift in the trajectory of the Smithsons' approach as well as a huge evolution in the development of attitudes toward modernism in Britain. When the Smithsons submitted their entry to the Hunstanton School competition in 1949, they were more adventurously modernist than their peers but still somewhat naively groping for a way forward. In the interval between then and 1954, when the project was completed and had been published in three major journals,[11] the status, understanding, and prospects of modern architecture in Britian were fundamentally and rapidly changing. So, too, were the Smithsons' response and outlook. By 1954, there were no longer many influential architects or critics who opposed modernism to British traditions. Rather, the pervasive question in the journals and at the Royal Institute of British Architects (RIBA) was how modernism could evolve uniquely in Britain, as is clear in Banham's 1953 article celebrating the beginning of the RIBA presidency of Howard Robertson (who began writing books on modern design in 1922, had been the first British representative to CIAM, and had served as a member of the design team for the United Nations) as the affirmation of modernism's acceptance by the British architectural establishment.[12] Perhaps most significant, disappointment about the "contemporary style" of the Festival of Britain in 1951 had provoked architects, artists, and designers to take principled stands on modernism, which found support at the recently founded (1946) ICA. By 1951, the ICA was fully established, flourishing, and influential. Divergent and dissenting views on modernism quickly emerged, and in 1952 the ICA began its sponsorship of the activities of a "young independent group" (soon to be known simply as the Independent Group, or IG), which would embrace popular media and American art and culture as well as far-ranging intellectual speculation on the future of art and design. Banham quickly assumed leadership of the IG, and under its umbrella the Smithsons were important collaborators with Henderson and Paolozzi not only on the *Parallel of Life and Art* show, but later on a project for the *This Is Tomorrow* exhibition as well (1956).

Thus, even as Hunstanton was under construction (and delayed by steel shortages) the Smithsons began to see their work in terms of photography, popular culture, advertising, and American movies. No sooner than they had decided to claim and revise the steel, glass, and brick idiom of Mies's Chicago work, the Smithsons were swept up in and by the IG. As a result, their interests and working methods expanded, and the power of Mies's example became less vivid in a scene that was dense with other more shocking or fresh sources, such as Henderson's "street" photography, Paolozzi's famous epidiascope lecture at the IG's first meeting, John McHale's love of American

85 VIEWS OF THE HUNSTANTON SECONDARY MODERN SCHOOL BY ALISON AND PETER SMITHSON UNDER CONSTRUCTION, 1953. THESE PHOTOGRAPHS WERE TAKEN BY NIGEL HENDERSON, A FRIEND AND COLLABORATOR OF THE SMITHSONS.

magazines, and Richard Hamilton's Duchampian sensibility. This shift in awareness between 1949 and 1954, and the Smithsons' decisions to document and publish the Hunstanton project in ways that drew on their new sensibilities and seemingly diverged from their original conception, play into the general and pervasive critique that they were persistently inconsistent and incoherent. For most, it reinforces the accepted wisdom that there is an irresolvable conflict between their initial, intense, dogged, contrarian, and idiosyncratic attempts to find, and found, a renewed, robust modern architecture that was as tangible and direct in its means as it was broad in its effects, and their subsequent fascination with popular culture and mass-media.

For example, Claire Zimmerman, in her recent essay "Photographic Images from Chicago to Hunstanton," argues precisely that point, claiming that the "new status of the image in building" after World War II required "asserting the value of spatial experience over media representation." To do otherwise, she suggests, is nothing less than an anticipation of post-modernism's ironies and its treatment of representation as a substitute for building, leading her to conclude that "for the Smithsons, the influence of media representation and dissemination on architecture required the most stringent architectural response, one that opposed the apparent reductions of media society with architecture capable of *defying the image, even through the image*."[13] Thus she, and most others who are now writing the history of New Brutalism, reinforce the premise that the efficacy and ethic of post-war modern architecture was compromised by a culture increasingly saturated by mass-media and image. But the story of the Smithsons' transit from the insistent directness of neo-modern New Brutalism as a means to engage the world to an understanding of ways to recast their own prior architectural propositions in terms of media and image might also suggest the promise of a future that had been emergent long before them (as media theorists like Walter Benjamin in the 1930s and Marshall McLuhan in the 1950s understood)[14] and which continues today without apparent paradox or reduction in our computational, automated, and mediated realities of production and exchange. Just as Mies is now understood in terms of media, effect and technologies of reproduction, New Brutalism's complex beginnings allow a similarly complex understanding of its motives and aspirations.

MODERNIST MIES

Certainly by 1954 it must have been difficult to remember why just a few years earlier, in the late 1940s, soon after the MoMA show brought widespread attention to Mies's Chicago practice and re-established Mies as a major contemporary figure with a vision for the future, the Smithsons' choice of Mies was so adventurous and shrewd. It not only allied them with American culture and building technology but also with an architect who was not well-known among British architects and seemingly had produced relatively little after emigrating from Germany in 1937. But unlike most of their peers, the Smithsons were certainly aware of Mies's German work of the 1920s (Johnson's MoMA catalogue included the glass skyscrapers and concrete office building that were published in the magazine *G* in the 1920s as well as the Weissenhof Settlement and his brick houses) and were quick to see the potential of the Chicago work, which must have appeared absolutely startling in comparison.

Yet the Chicago Mies would reverberate uncertainly in British assessments of modernism. For example, the 1962 edition of J. M. Richards's popular Penguin paperback, *Modern Architecture* (first edition, 1932), not only featured the Minerals and Metals Research Building on its cover, but the plates, plans, and descriptions of the Barcelona Pavilion and Tugendhat House that had appeared in earlier editions were replaced with Mies's Chicago projects, and the text discussed the newer buildings as exemplars of his work. However, Richards did not advance an interpretation of Mies aligned with New Brutalism. Rather, he reiterated the caricature of Mies as simultaneously "rational and matter-of-fact"[15] and a poet of building technology. Richards described the buildings at IIT and the Lakeshore Drive towers as

masterpieces of precise engineering, devoid of ornament, or of qualities (such as those arising from the effects of the weather or from the varying textures of materials) that cannot be precisely controlled. They rely for their aesthetic effect on subtlety of proportion and mechanical precision of finish.[16]

According to Richards, the Chicago projects are "precise, logical studies in pure geometry,"[17] yet Mies "can transform the cold mechanical rhythms which arise from these methods into a quite magical feeling for the interplay of enclosed and semi-enclosed space,"[18] thereby "evoking the same sort of aesthetic satisfaction as a neatly balanced mathematical equation."[19]

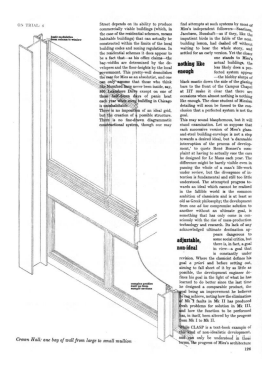

Crown Hall: one bay of wall from large to small mullion

PAGE FROM REYNER BANHAM, "ON TRIAL: MIES VAN DER ROHE. ALMOST NOTHING IS TOO MUCH," *ARCHITECTURAL REVIEW*, AUGUST 1962.

Banham had an entirely different evaluation of Mies at that time. In the concluding chapter of *Theory and Design in the First Machine Age* (1960) he discusses the Barcelona Pavilion as a departure from the strident claims and polemical strictures of the *G* era and the beginning of a "purely symbolic"[20] aesthetic aligned with the International Style. For Banham, the Barcelona Pavilion exemplifies the unfortunate swerve from functionalism and "technological culture" that was the fate of the architecture of the first machine age. But his most provocative criticism of the time addresses Mies's Chicago work. In his article on Mies in his 1962 "On Trial" series in *Architectural Review*, he argues that Mies's genius can indeed be found in the details, but it is a "peculiar authority"[21] that derives from ingenuity and a willingness to "define his goal in the light of what he has learned to do better since the last time he designed a comparable product"[22] and in light of available technology. It is as if Banham is suggesting that in Chicago, Mies recuperated some aspects of his Dada-affiliated ethos from the *G* years, as expressed in his famous statement: "We reject all aesthetic speculation, all doctrine, all formalism."[23] In Chicago, Mies's anti-aesthetic was manifest as pragmatic R&D prototyping, in the manner of a hot-rod tinkerer whose work is "built up from catalogued parts and adapters."[24] Banham's 1962 Mies is the master of prosaic technologies like the suspended ceiling[25] and is, in fact, a practical imperfectionist, a claim Banham makes stridently and vividly:

Mies van der Rohe: Seagram Building, New York, 1958 (at right, Lever House; centre, behind church, spire), the Racquet Club.

Philip Johnson's partnership with Mies van der Rohe on the Seagram building was the culmination of a master/pupil relationship based, in the first instance, on a scholarly admiration for Mies's work. Born in 1906, Johnson was almost forty before he even trained as an architect, but was already established as a critic and propagandist of 'The International Style' – a term he and the historian Henry-Russell Hitchcock had used to title their pioneering book on the aesthetics of modern architecture in 1933. His own career as an architect has been notable, but he may well be longest remembered as a Modern architecture's sharpest wit and raconteur.

Skidmore, Owings and Merrill have only become the life, soul and epitome of big business architecture since the beginning of the fifties. An immense and reliable design-organisation even before that date, they still needed the undoubted talents of Gordon Bunshaft (born 1904) who joined the firm in 1946, to propel them to the forefront of the US and world scenes. With Lever House, in 1952, SOM and Bunshaft made a permanent mark, and entered on a career that transcended the limitations of big business architecture with such works as the US Air Force Academy at Colorado Springs.

Few architectural confrontations can be as fascinating, or as inscrutable, as that between the Seagram Building and the Racquet Club, facing one another across Park Avenue, and Lever House, oblique from Seagram but flanking the Racquet Club. The club is a most expert exercise in Beaux-Arts expertise by McKim, Meade and White, the American partnership who showed the French in the nineties that the Ecole des Beaux-Arts could be beaten at its own game of brilliant cliché-mongering. The Racquet Club is an *exercice de style*, and a skill in resolving visual problems that still strikes a chord in the architects of today.

Indeed, this trialogue is a discourse upon style in the grandest manner, in which the club puts down a basic proposition of traditional skill, and the other two discourse upon it in modern terms, derived from New York's first true dream, the UN Secretariat. UN was a European dream, the glass tower set between city and water, and planted in a townscape where skyscrapers are not a dream but a dirty commercial reality. The contrast between the ideal and the real set off

a brisk discussion on the aesthetics of the skyscraper in New York. Lever and Seagram are the two most authoritative statements made, in built fact, in that discussion.

Gordon Bunshaft, the most brilliant designer to practice under the S O M umbrella, clearly set out to Americanise the European dream represented by UN, by imparting a dash of the puritanical – Lever is glazed all round, UN only on the main facades – more conspicuously public-spirited: Lever is flanked by a little piazza 'dedicated to the public use'. Unwittingly or clairvoyantly, Bunshaft built a monument to an America whose existence could barely be sensed at the time: Eisenhower America, grey-flannel-suit America, with Madison Avenue literally only a block away. Its smoothly elegant assurance was typically a compromise between two great creative ideas – Le Corbusier's vision of the tall slab with auxiliary structures at its foot, and Mies van der Rohe's vision of the all-glass tower. It gave architectural expression to an age just as the age was being born, and while the age lasted', or its standards persisted, Lever House was an uncontrollable success, imitated and sometimes understood all over the Americanised world, and one of the sights of New York.

But it was not what many observers believed it to be at the time, the last word in glass boxes. Over in Chicago, Mies van der Rohe was steadily developing his aesthetic (or was it a structural *rationale*?) of refined purity and rectilinear structural expression to a point of seeming logic well beyond the craftsmanly compromise of Lever House, and in the mid-fifties – rather suddenly, following some brisk internal intrigue among the Bronfman (Seagram) clan – Mies van der Rohe and his most devoted follower, Philip Johnson, found themselves designing an office block almost opposite Lever House.

But not dead opposite, and the first acknowledgement that the Seagram makes to any of its neighbours is to the Racquet Club. Standing back a little haughtily from the

pavement, it takes care to share the same axis as the club, each standing symmetrically about the entrances that exactly face one another. This kind of formal good manners is Old World (not to say Olde Worlde) and quite un-American, and at every turn the Seagram reveals a kind of sophistication, an approach to urbanism, that has more in common with the Europe-oriented architecture directly in front of it, than with Bunshaft's unmistakably All-American Lever House standing catty-corner to the right. Lever stands well up to the pavement, but its slab is shoulder-on to the road. Seagram stands back, and front-on to the Avenue. Lever plays up glassiness, transparency and reflection, but Seagram, surprisingly, does not, emphasising instead the solidity of its block form, using a tinted glass that is darker and browner than Lever's, and bronze mullions that stick out from the facade as positively as pilasters, whereas the stainless steel glazing-bars at Lever barely ripple the surface, while the actual proportion of the tall narrow windows above the bronze spandrel panels (Lever has glass spandrels) recalls the fenestration of ancient palazzi.

Seagram and Lever have now been imitated to the point of tedium: 'square glass boxes' are a drug on the commercial market all over the world. Few of these imitators have had space, wit, or finance to pursue the piazza theme however: the Civic Center in Chicago by C F Murphy and Associates is the most noble exception to this depressing rule. If one seeks a true development of this concept of commercial public space it is most notably found in a work by two of Mies's more remote admirers. The crop-cornered towers that cluster around a raised pedestrian yard off St James's Street in London's clubland to form the premises of that grand old weekly paper *The Economist*, are the work of Alison and Peter Smithson. Their early reputation depended on a building that frankly imitated Mies – the school at Hunstanton – but their pursuit of their ever-admired master became less and less obvious, and at *The Economist* the tell-tale traces tend to lurk half-hidden, like the metal sections behind the stone facing of the columns.

Alison and Peter Smithson (born 1928 and 1923 respectively) are now the most internationally renowned husband-and-wife team working in Britain. Their reputation is based on a sparse roster of stern but controversial buildings, beginning with their Miesian-looking school at Hunstanton (see p 128). At the time the school was being finished they enunciated their philosophy as 'The New Brutalism' – a phrase which scandalised the Establishment (as it was meant to do) but enshrined a solid architectural morality to which students and younger architects turned for support not available elsewhere in the Fifties.

The groupings of these three towers (plus the matching monumental bay window on the never-before-exposed side wall of Boodles club) around a small piazza is – among other things – an attempt to develop the rather diagrammatic concept of fore-court demonstrated at Seagram into a more active contribution to the life and townscape of an area that is much more complex than Park Avenue. To move forward from Mies, the Smithsons were prepared to take a long step backward, to return to the sources of the Classical tradition that was always the backbone of Mies's designing. They know and love the sacred sites of ancient Greece; they have views on how and why they were planned as they were. Any visitor who stands at the foot of the steps that rise from St James's Street to the piazza and compares the grouping of the buildings with what he can remember of the view up to the Acropolis of Athens through the Propylaea may decide that what he sees could be the subtlest and craftiest piece of learning from Antiquity this century has produced.

Alison and Peter Smithson: *Economist Buildings, London, 1964*

114   115

88   SPREAD FROM REYNER BANHAM, *THE AGE OF THE MASTERS*, 1975.

The closer one stands to Mies's actual buildings, the less likely does a perfected system appear – the blobby slurps of black mastic down the side of the glazing bars to the front of the Campus Chapel at IIT make it clear that there are occasions when almost nothing is nothing like enough. The close student of Miesian detailing will soon be forced to the conclusion that a perfected system is not the goal. This may sound blasphemous, but it will stand examination.[26]

In the same year, Banham's *Guide to Modern Architecture* offers a similar, if tempered, characterization of Mies. The book ends with a presentation of IIT's Crown Hall and the conclusion that the abstractness of the structure produces "sheer space," which forces us to "fix on the details" that join steel to glass. Those joints "work" but are not "the final and perfect joint" and never will be. They are the "best-possible solutions for today" and "it is in details such as those at Crown Hall, perfected today but perfectible tomorrow, that one sees what kind of God is modern architecture's."[27]

MASTER MIES

When the *Guide to Modern Architecture* was revised and republished in 1975 Banham did not alter his examples, arguments, or assessment of Mies. But he did amend them in ways that revised his historical narrative: first, by reviving the affiliation of Mies and New Brutalism and, second, by recuperating his 1955 position that the New Brutalist aim to redirect modernism was not fulfilled by the Smithsons' decision to emulate Mies.

Crown Hall, interior

Crown Hall, detailing of main frame

Alison and Peter Smithson: *secondary school, Hunstanton, 1954*

89   VIEWS OF CROWN HALL AT IIT BY LUDWIG MIES VAN DER ROHE AND THE HUNSTANTON SECONDARY MODERN SCHOOL BY ALISON AND PETER SMITHSON IN REYNER BANHAM, *THE AGE OF THE MASTERS*, 1975.

The 1975 book was retitled, *The Age of The Masters*, and Banham was more explicit than ever in his characterization of Mies as the master of "the True Style." This back-handed compliment tagged Mies as the greatest of modern architects but also always a representative of the past. To acclaim Mies as a "Master" meant that he was not, and never could have been, a vital source for the next generation. If in 1955 Mies was banished by Banham in favor of other sources for New Brutalism, Banham's return to Mies in the 1960s and 1970s is part and parcel of his ambivalent judgment that New Brutalism was truly ambitious, though not as forward-looking as it may have seemed. That argument first appears in Banham's 1966 book, *The New Brutalism: Ethic or Aesthetic?*, where he writes: "the Smithsons [and] all others who could carry the name of Brutalist [...] are dedicated to the traditions of architecture as the world has come to know them: their aim is not *'une architecture autre'* but, as ever, *'vers une architecture.'*"[28] Thus, it was only after New Brutalism was no longer an ongoing movement, and then again after Mies's death, that direct connections between Mies and New Brutalism returned to Banham's accounts and explanations. In 1975, most importantly, Banham explicitly acknowledged the significance of Mies's influence on the Smithsons and the historical significance of the Smithsons' choice. While there are no projects by the Smithsons in the 1962 book, the 1975 revision includes two of their projects, and each is paired with one of the Mies buildings that appeared in the first version. The Economist Complex (1959–1964) is added to Banham's comparison of the Seagram Building and Gordon Bunshaft's Lever House, while an image of Hunstanton is included with those of Crown Hall.[29]

Yet it took a few years to crystallize in the minds of the Smithsons, and when it finally did, their connections with the academic rationalists were becoming tenuous.

Nevertheless, in spite of this, the New Brutalism was definitely in the academic tradition of calculated 'movements'. This is clear from the Smithsons' first building, Hunstanton School [152], which is full of historical

152. Alison and Peter Smithson: Hunstanton School, Hunstanton, 1949-54. The formal ordering is academic, both Palladian and Miesian, but the underlying attitude is ascetic and literalist: bricks are bricks, steel is steel and never a metaphor shall they become. Except Brutalist.

references. Yet the deeper characteristics were quite original in tone. All the materials were used 'as found' without trying to become metaphors for other materials. In this sense Brutalism was never more than a dramatization of honest literalism: it argued that things taken in themselves are more honest and evocative than any anthropomorphic meanings which may have become attached. In short the metaphor of literalism. However, Hunstanton did also have explicit reference to past works, to the Miesian idiom of frame and infill and to the Palladian order of rectilinear formality. It was this latter allusion which was most apparent to the rationalists.

251

90   PAGE FROM CHARLES JENCKS, *MODERN MOVEMENTS IN ARCHITECTURE*, 1971.

MORE MIESES

Banham's 1975 revisions were a late entry in an ongoing discourse in the late 1960s and early 1970s when Banham, the Smithsons, and Banham's heretical student Charles Jencks engaged in a vibrant contestation of modernism's identity and legacy, its promise or its failure, through their divergent evaluations of Mies and explicit connections to New Brutalism. Following the completion of the Smithsons' Economist

Complex, which was judged by many, including Banham, to mark the end of New Brutalism (in part because of its embrace of the more formal and classicizing aspects of Mies), the Smithsons offered their most explicit and original interpretations of Mies: first in their 1965 "Heroic Period of Modern Architecture" edition of *Architectural Design* and then in a 1967 seminar in Berlin, which would be published as an homage to Mies one month before he died, and revised once again for inclusion in *Without Rhetoric* (1974).[30] The Mies that the Smithsons emulated was "surprisingly tuned-in to our culture": an ingenious exemplar of "repetition as a quality in itself" and "ordered sameness" who understood how to assert fundamental architectural coherence and integrity in a mass-production society. "With Mies, repetition is life-including, his feeling for it can make the multiplied thing magical in its very multiplication." They saw this in two aspects of his work, beginning as early as 1919 in the Friedrichstrasse office buildings: "an almost autonomouos, repetitive, neutralizing skin" and "a recessive, calm, green, urban pattern."[31]

Meanwhile, Charles Jencks saw Mies's work as the epitome of impoverished modern dogmas. His 1971 book, *Modern Movements in Architecture* (which was based on his thesis advised by Banham at London University), establishes the basic semiotic premise that architecture must be multivalent. He launches this argument in the second chapter, "The Problem of Mies," by framing Mies as a negative example of "univalent literalism" and "reductivism" who "demands an absolute commitment to the Platonic world-view in order to appreciate his buildings."[32] According to Jencks, "critics and architects are prepared to inhabit this world as if it were complete: none more so than Peter and Alison Smithson."[33] Later in the book Jencks returns to this accusation and his example is none other than New Brutalism and the Hunstanton School: "Brutalism was never more than a dramatiza-tion of honest literalism," he writes, and in the caption of a photograph of Hunstanton that clearly references similar photographs of the Minerals and Metals Research Building at IIT, Jencks adds: "The formal ordering is academic, both Palladian and Miesian, but the underlying attitude is ascetic and literalist: bricks are bricks, steel is steel and never a metaphor they shall become. Except Brutalist."[34]

BRUTALIST MIES

What can be learned from Mies's uncertain status in British modernism between 1950 and 1975? How does Mies, and how do Banham's and the Smithsons' varied attempts to come to terms with Mies at different times and in different contexts, provide evidence not only for understanding New Brutalism, but also for understanding the trajectories that were particular to British modernism? Are Banham's Mieses an underestimation of Mies's influence that too quickly discounts the Smithsons' first Miesian insights? Might the Smithsons' hunch that the Chicago Mies could sustain a modernist counter-movement have been astute and wise, even if the ambition was seemingly unrealized?

Have the last two decades of recuperations of Mies proved the characterizations of both Banham and Jencks too limited? Is there a newer New Brutalism that is rediscovering the Smithsons' insights, or potential insights, regarding Mies?

These questions suggest an understanding of New Brutalism that diverges from those histories that track the Smithsons' development from Hunstanton (where Mies is primarily a curious, convenient, aberrant starting point for the movement) through their involvement in the Independent Group and their leadership of Team X to their major projects of the 1960s, such as the Economist Complex and Robin Hood Gardens in London. Instead of insisting on the Smithsons' idiosyncratic and inconsistent approaches to various projects at different times, it may be that tracking the status of Mies as a persistent influence allows a re-evaluation of the premises and promises of New Brutalism.[35] In fact, tracking Mies's appearance in the explanations, revisions, and recollections of New Brutalism may produce some clarity for a movement that has never allowed a coherent, principled, or narrative accounting of itself.

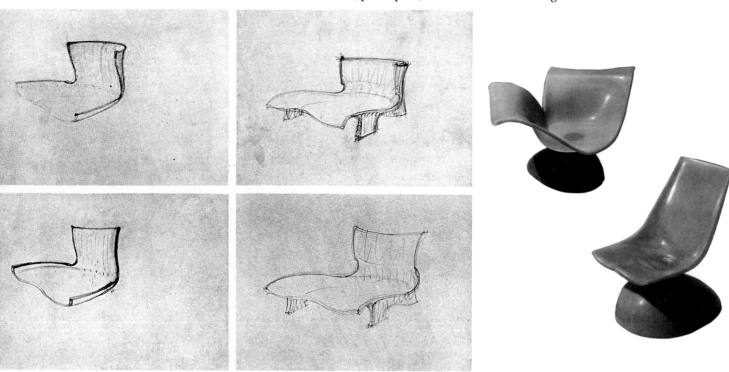

92 LEFT: LUDWIG MIES VAN DER ROHE, SKETCHES FOR "CONCHOIDAL" CHAIRS, EARLY 1940S.
RIGHT: ALISON AND PETER SMITHSON, "TULIP" AND "EGG" CHAIRS FOR THE HOUSE OF THE FUTURE, 1956.

A quarter-century of arguments about, and uses of, Mies in British architecture reveals not only an unfamiliar Mies seen through the lens of British politics and intellectual culture, but also alternative visions of modernist architecture and new insights into the intentions of New Brutalism, inspired as it was by Mies's work in Chicago as well as American culture generally. Studying New Brutalism opens up a historical condition that still codes its complexity and is not contained by either the projects of particular architects or the contemporary and retrospective attempts to characterize it, or theorize it. Yet the specific question of how Mies inspired a movement that has come to be associated with massive, reinforced concrete buildings is a curious story (although it is not difficult to view Mies's Concrete Office Building project as proto-brutal) that helps illuminate new understandings of British modernism and Mies's Chicago practice. The story of the unresolved status of Mies in British modernism is one strand of the now pervasive understanding of Mies as an enigma upon whom we can project multiple readings of modernism. There is a New Brutalist Mies that remains to be understood.

NOTES

[1] The *Architects' Journal* of January 3, 1946, included four pages of photographs and drawings of the Minerals and Metals Research Building and five pages of drawings of the Library and Administration Building, though Peter Smithson says he first saw the pages, cut from the magazine, only after Alison, then in London, sent them to him in 1949 when he was still at school in Newcastle. The couple had purchased the Philip Johnson monograph earlier that year. The book has similar images to the article, plus photographs of Alumni Memorial Hall, a photo of the steel-frame of the Chemistry Building under construction, and drawings of several other proposed buildings at IIT. See Peter Smithson, "Reflections on Hunstanton," *ARQ 2* (Summer 1997), p. 35.

[2] The Tugendhat House was featured in both F. R. S. Yorke, *The Modern House* (London: The Architectural Press, 1934) and J. M. Richards, *An Introduction to Modern Architecture* (London: Pelican, 1940), and the Barcelona Pavilion in the latter.

[3] The fundamental tension during the Labour government of Clement Atlee (1945–1951) was between those who advocated the development of a progressive social welfare state and internationalism in culture and politics, and those who were committed to restoring British traditional cultural values and society.

[4] As Mark Crinson explains, the culture of post-war Britain was "veering back and forth between the experience of austerity and deindustrialization on the one hand and a selected sense of affluence and American-style consumerism on the other." Mark Crinson, " 'A House which Grows': Stirling and Gowan, the Smithsons, and Consumer Society," in M. Crinson and C. Zimmerman, eds., *Neo-Avant-Garde and Postmodern: Postwar Architecture in Britain and Beyond* (New Haven: Yale University Press, 2010), p. 177.

[5] For a detailed account of British architectural publications, see Andrew Higgott, *Mediating Modernity: Architectural Culture in Britain* (Oxford: Routledge, 2006). On modernism's emergence in Britain, see for example Nicholas Bullock, *Building the Post-War World: Modern Architecture and Reconstruction in Britain* (Oxford: Routledge, 2002), and Elizabeth Darling, *Re-Forming Britain: Narratives of Modernity before Reconstruction* (Oxford: Routledge, 2007).

[6] See Stephen Kite, "Softs and Hards: Colin St. John Wilson and the Contested Visions of 1950s London" in *Neo-Avant-Garde and Postmodern*, pp. 62 and 72.

[7] Reyner Banham, "The New Brutalism," *Architectural Review*, 118 (December 1955), pp. 355–361.

[8] Ibid., p. 358.

[9] Banham claims that the "concept of the *Image* is common to all aspects of The New Brutalism in England.

[...] Basically, it requires that the building should be an immediately graspable visual entity, and that the form grasped by the eye should be confirmed by experience of the building in use." Banham, "The New Brutalism," p. 358.

[10] Banham, "The New Brutalism," p. 361.

[11] Extensive documentation of Hunstanton was published in the three preeminent British journals: *Architects' Journal*, 118 (September 10, 1953), pp. 323–328, *Architectural Design* (September 1953), pp. 238–348, and *Architectural Review*, 116 (September 1954), pp. 149–162.

[12] Reyner Banham, "Howard Robertson," *Architectural Review* (September 1953), pp. 161–168.

[13] Claire Zimmerman, "Photographic Images from Chicago to Hunstanton," in *Neo-Avant-Garde and Postmodern*, pp. 207–208.

[14] The Independent Group was unaware of Benjamin, but did take an interest in McLuhan's *The Mechanical Bride: Folklore of Industrial Man*, published in 1951.

[15] Richards, *An Introduction to Modern Architecture*, p. 85.

[16] Ibid., p. 110.

[17] Ibid., p. 87.

[18] Ibid., p. 111.

[19] Ibid., p. 158.

[20] Reyner Banham, *Theory and Design in the First Machine Age* (Cambridge, MA: MIT Press, 1980), p. 321.

[21] Reyner Banham, "On Trial: Mies van der Rohe: Almost Nothing Is Too Much," *Architectural Review* (August 1962), p. 128.

[22] Ibid., p. 126.

[23] Quoted in Banham, *Theory and Design in the First Machine Age*, p. 271. The original quotation appears in the first issue of *G* (July 1923), while the translation matches that in Philip Johnson's book.

[24] Banham, "On Trial: Mies van der Rohe: Almost Nothing Is Too Much," p. 126. Banham explains: "The development from one ad hoc compromise solution to another without an ultimate goal, is something that has come in only with the rise of mass-production technology and research."

[25] Banham offers the example of the suspended ceiling in the first article of the "On Trial" series. Reyner Banham, "On Trial: The Situation: What Architecture of Technology?" *Architectural Review* (February 1962), p. 99.

[26] Banham, "On Trial: Mies van der Rohe: Almost Nothing Is Too Much," p. 126.

[27] Reyner Banham, *Guide to Modern Architecture* (London: Architectural Press, 1962), p. 154.

[28] Reyner Banham, *The New Brutalism: Ethic or Aesthetic?* (New York: Reinhold Publishing Corp., 1966), p. 69.

[29] A third Mies building was added in the 1975 book, the Berlin National Gallery, unpaired with a project by the Smithsons, as the conclusion of the book and replacing Crown Hall as the exemplar of mastery.

[30] "The Heroic Period of Modern Architecture" first appeared as the December 1965 issue of *Architectural Design*. The 1967 seminar was held in December at the Technische Universität Berlin and published as "Mies van der Rohe," *Architectural Design* (July 1969), pp. 363–366, as well as in a somewhat different form in the book, *Without Rhetoric: An Architectural Aesthetic*, 1955–1972 (Cambridge, MA: MIT Press, 1974).

[31] Alison and Peter Smithson, "Mies van der Rohe," *Architectural Design* (July 1969), pp. 363, 365, 366.

[32] Charles Jencks, *Modern Movements in Architecture* (New York: Anchor Press, 1971), pp. 22, 95.

[33] Ibid., p. 98.

[34] Ibid., p. 251. Most important, Jencks sets up the Smithsons, as exemplified by Hunstanton and the Economist Complex, as the opposite of the Pop architecture that he celebrates, thus reinforcing the irreconcilability of the Smithsons' Miesian New Brutalism and their involvement in the Independent Group. On at least this Banham and Jencks agree.

[35] See for example Mies's "Conchoidal" plastic chairs in Johnson's monograph of 1946 (pp. 172–173) as prototypes for the Smithsons' furniture in their House of the Future (1956).

AMERICAN AESTHETIC

KAZYS VARNELIS

Towering over Chicago like a rocket on a launch pad, the John Hancock Center is a work of architectural science fiction. Contemporaneous with the Saturn V, "Big John" shares the same faith in a technological future. Technology shapes the building; its aluminum-clad trussed tube, developed by engineer Fazlur Kahn, withstands strong wind without heavy interior shear walls. The antennas surmounting it recall the Saturn V's escape towers.

If we associate the revitalization of city centers with creativity, fashion, and a walkable scale today, the John Hancock Center provides an alternate history in which engineering and megastructures were to revive the core. While the one hundred-story stacked tower cost more than a conventional two-building solution, it realized gains from having the highest residences on Earth. The tower's population can commute by elevator from their upper-story apartments to offices below – effectively, living in a "city within a city." But the building also established a vertical suburbia downtown. Although residents were captivated by the lake, clouds, and migrating birds, they lived disconnected from the city below, which receded into an abstract background. With an interior pool, gym, restaurants, and shops, the building's developers bragged that one would never have to leave the structure. The sunken plaza separating the ground floor from Michigan Avenue only heightened this disconnection, emphasizing that the privileged entrance is from a concrete spiral ramp bringing cars up to the interior parking deck.

SOM founder Nathaniel Owings explained that introducing suburban ease at unprecedented densities in the city would curb sprawl. A homegrown counterpart to Archigram, "Big John" emphatically announced the return of the urban core under the sign of

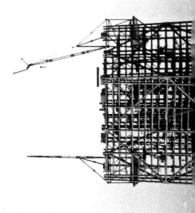

technology. Today, we again embrace technology, but our ambition is tempered. Gazing at the vector that is the John Hancock Center, how can we fail to dream big again?

JOHN HANCOCK CENTER, SKIDMORE, OWINGS & MERRILL, 1970.

TITANIC RISING

The Vietnam War, the oil crisis, the Carter presidency, Crown Hall: they were all the result of technological overreach. Towards the end of the century in which we believed that we could rationalize every aspect of human life, turning us into machines, "human potential," cannon fodder, or, as Martin Heidegger put it, "standing reserve," we realized that instead of reaching perfection, we were approaching self-destruction. In Stanley Tigerman's 1978 collage, *The Titanic*, one of architecture's most utopian symbols, not just of perfection but also of autonomous self-refinement, sinks like the titanic overreach in glass and steel architecture it was. Instead of the centralized – and not very comfortable – focal point of a factory complex designed to produce architects who would in turn reproduce its own almost-perfect forms, it becomes a fragment. It is a remnant that now acts like a piece of spolia out of which Tigerman creates a new kind of architecture.

For *The Titanic* is not just a critique. It is a building block. It builds an architecture that is part aqueous fluidity, part fragment, part dynamic diagonal, and all a re-using of what already exists. It is post-modern in the most fundamental sense of that word. It is not so much commentary as it is a strategic proposal. Ever since *The Titanic* and its kin, from *Delirious New York* and *Manhattan Transcripts* to Frank Gehry's studs, chain-link fence, and folds borrowed from baroque sculpture, we have known that what we make today is a gathering together of what exists, as idea and as practice. It represents a sane approach to our reality exactly in its seeming refusal at logic.

This Titanic is not sinking. It is rising, like a submarine, out of our shared past to help build a more sane, if un-stable and uncertain, future.

THE TITANIC, STANLEY TIGERMAN, 1978.

MEGALOPOLIS IS EVERYWHERE

ALBERT POPE

TIPPING POINT

The 2010 census brought some interesting facts to light concerning urban trends in the Chicago Metropolitan Area. Despite the appearance of new high-profile projects within and adjacent to the city center, the rate of people moving out of the city continues to increase at a steady pace. Since the population peaked in 1950, the city of Chicago has shown a net loss of almost a million people. These population declines have of course been offset by population gains in what the census bureau calls the "outer suburbs," making Chicago today one of the most sparsely populated large cities in the country and in the world. To say the least, this reality is strikingly at odds with the city's celebrated urban reputation.

The facts spelled out in the 2010 census are generally known, but they are far from understood. While everyone is vaguely aware that Chicago is a highly dispersed urban sprawl, growing ever larger with each successive census, most continue to think of its tiny, statistically negligible urban core as representative of the city overall. This

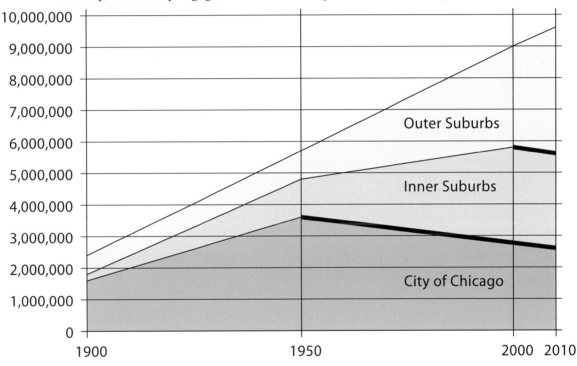

CHICAGO METROPOLITAN REGION, 1900–2010, SHARE OF POPULATION DEFINED BY CENSUS SECTOR. LUDWIG HILBERSEIMER ARRIVED IN CHICAGO AT THE PEAK OF ITS GROWTH AND SPENT THE REST OF HIS CAREER RIDING THE DOWNSLOPE OF THE CITY IN WHICH HE LIVED AND WORKED.

misconception is verified by the commonplace references to the vast bulk of Chicago's extent as suburban. This habit of speech stands in striking contrast to the fact that the majority (seventy-five percent) of the city's population can hardly stand as parasite to a minority host. This is especially true when that majority is constituted by autonomous, fully functioning urban environments. In what sense are the social, political, and economic interests of Schaumburg, for example, subordinate to those interests residing inside the Loop? What the census makes clearer with each passing decade is that the urban reality in which we live has long outstripped the very words we employ to understand it. Urban, suburban, center, periphery, Metropolis, even the term City itself, no longer correspond to existing urban realities. Yet, we continue to employ these habits of speech and thought despite all evidence to the contrary.

This confusion applies of course to every major city in North America, even those in the South with far less traditional urban substance than Chicago. Yet, in Chicago, it seems even less defensible because of the remarkable role the city has played in the development of modern urban history. While approximately twenty-five percent of the metropolitan population lives within the city limits, and a far smaller percentage inside the Loop, it is not an understatement to say that one hundred percent of the urban and architectural interest lies in this relatively small part of the city. Like the doctor who declares a patient healthy based solely on the whiteness of his teeth, the vast bulk of the city is too frequently overpowered by the brilliant smile of, say, the Trump International Hotel and Tower, a Frank Gehry folly, or the latest museum addition by Renzo Piano. And it is not a case of temporary blindness. The seventy-five percent of the urban substance that lies outside the city limits is not simply ignored but remains "unseen" owing to the lack of clear concepts capable of rendering it visible. Long forgotten, the most important of these concepts were hatched in and for Chicago.

Once upon a time, Beaux-Arts architects limited their interest in the city to the production of public monuments and the occasional mansion or tomb. Central to the idea of modern urbanism is the belief that an architect's obligation to the city goes beyond these traditional limits to include the entire city and all of its inhabitants, not just exceptional programs and their patrons. In Chicago, the formulation of new urban concepts that not only kept up with, but actually anticipated contemporary urban development has been an integral part of its urban history, a history that is tied directly to the city's remarkable growth in the nineteenth century and its even more remarkable transformation in the twentieth. The power of Chicago's example to the world was almost never, however, identified with rarefied programs and monumental expression. City Beautiful notwithstanding, Chicago architects engaged the post-war world by providing templates for the new type of urban development that would ultimately succeed the grid, street-and-block paradigm. One would like to include Olmsted's Riverside development (1869) as precursor to Wright's many suburban endeavors leading up to the formulation of Broadacre City (1932), but it was after World War II that the most imaginative and progressive work on modern urbanism began. One only needs to recall the work of Ludwig Mies van der Rohe and Ludwig Hilberseimer at Lafayette Park (1956), Walter Netsch at the University of Illinois at Chicago Circle (1965), and Bertrand Goldberg at River City (1972) to name but four Chicago architects who were actively creating distinctive alternatives to gridiron urbanism.

This important chapter of modern urban history was largely buried under the neoliberal critique of modern urbanism that took place in the 1970s. The post-modern and anti-modern rejection of modern urbanism–as influential today as it ever was–forced architects to retreat into the relatively modest preoccupations of renewing and renovating traditional cities, leaving aside anything that did not fit into traditional street-and-block templates. Now that seventy-five percent of the city does not fit into such templates, the question of relevance cannot be avoided. Can designers claim to know and to serve the city when that knowledge and service only extends to twenty-five percent of its substance? In other words, what constitutes the suburb's critical mass? Is it possible to remain focused on street-and-block aggregation while the vast majority of urban substance grows by entirely different protocols? We are indeed looking at a tipping point. In the meantime, a reconsideration of Chicago's unique contribution to post-war urbanism is clearly in order. To that end, I will focus this study on the work of just one of its visionary architects – Ludwig Hilberseimer – who spent the majority of his academic career ruminating on the fate of his adopted hometown.

DISAGGREGATION

At the midpoint of the twentieth century, the great post-war expansion was under-way and already producing staggering effects. The powerful and seductively new political economy that the war had brought into existence was already shutting down the complex protocols of urban production that had brought the city to its peak. Relocating the site of urban production and radically changing its specifications, this new economy broke the back of the traditional forms of block-by-block aggregation. Nowhere would the shock of this unprecedented retooling be more apparent than at the center of one of the most productive city-building machines in urban history.

Chicago was the Shenzhen of its day, growing from zero to three-and-a-half million people in its first one hundred years. Yet sometime between 1940 and 1950 the growth rate of the city peaked and then, remarkably, began to decline. The technical, economic, and political protocols responsible for a seemingly endless production of city blocks and a seemingly end-less extension of gridiron streets had suddenly come to a screeching halt, leaving the site of a century's progress to an immediate and precipitous decline. (The rate of Chicago's post-war population decline would turn out to nearly match the rate of its rapid ascent.) After 1950 the region of course continued to grow, but the gridiron streets and its large 300 by 600 foot blocks that once defined the City of Chicago would ultimately give way to closed, cul-de-sac expansion employing a completely different pattern of development at a significantly larger scale. The platting of Chicago's blocks and streets that began in 1830 would come to a decisive end in the second half of the twentieth century. The elements that defined Chicago's breakneck urban expansion were replaced, almost overnight, by a new set of urban protocols that are as different from blocks and streets as a Beaux-Arts monument is from the buildings of Mies van der Rohe.

Ludwig Hilberseimer had a front row seat to this dramatic reversal of Chicago's urban engine. He had immigrated to Chicago in 1938 to teach at the architecture school directed by Ludwig Mies van der Rohe, his colleague from the Berlin Bauhaus. Unlike Frank Lloyd Wright who lived and worked in elysium – the two bucolic fantasies (in Wisconsin and Arizona) he named Taliesin – or Le Corbusier who worked in the historic center of Paris, Hilberseimer worked and lived in the trenches of urban change.

As a result, it is no surprise that he was never content with idyllic new towns or urban nostalgia, but instead recognized disaggregation as a key element in the ongoing urban dynamic. Teaching at the Illinois Institute of Technology located in Chicago's Near South Side, Hilberseimer observed the urban fabric surrounding IIT literally disaggregate around him. Like a nuclear physicist working in a laboratory in Hiroshima, Hilberseimer witnessed the ground zero of modern urbanization and the seemingly catastrophic effects it brought down upon the traditional blocks and streets that surrounded the campus.

Hilberseimer knew the disaggregation of the Near South Side to be an extreme case of what was happening, at a much slower and less dramatic pace, in cities across North America. Coming after what was perhaps the most remarkable campaign of block-by-block urban expansion in the history of the world, the decline of the urban fabric of the Near South Side amounted to a breakdown of a seemingly unstoppable process. The immediate problem for anyone operating in the midst of this breakdown

104 MIES VAN DER ROHE AND HILBERSEIMER CELEBRATING THE END OF TERM WITH STUDENTS AT THE CHICAGO ART INSTITUTE STUDIO, DECEMBER, 1942. NOTE THE FOUR "SETTLEMENT UNITS" FROM HILBERSEIMER'S PLANNING STUDIO THAT ARE PAINTED ON THE WALL BEHIND MIES (LEFT).

was how to control the sudden effects of inner-city disaggregation. Desperate as the situation was, the spread of urban blight over hundreds of blocks was not an isolated problem but part of a larger picture. Hilberseimer's reputation as the twentieth century's preeminent urban theorist rides largely on the recognition and description of this larger picture.

Every American city has its own story to tell about the consequences of catastrophic urban decline. The stories are legend, from the Near South Side to the

South Bronx, from St. Louis to the entire District of Columbia, and include just about every provincial city whose central business district imploded in the early 1970s.

The details of each case are wrenching and one is loath to generalize given the painful details of each and every instance of urban decline. In the 1960s and 1970s, planners were so busy putting out fires that no one really bothered to think through why and how the fire started, how long it would burn and, most important, what relation the outbreak of blight might have to the explosive production of office parks, subdivisions, and shopping malls at the urban periphery. In effect, the very idea that an identifiable urban dynamic was in play and that this dynamic could be isolated and explained was lost on most architects, who just wanted to survive the upheaval and move on.

The identification of the larger and more abstract forces at play in this process is the job of urban theory. While many believe that cities evolve through a complex negotiation of strictly local contingencies, theorists realize that larger, more comprehensive forces affect the deployment of urban forms, linking together the operation of drastically different locales. At his particular historical juncture, and from his front row perspective on the Near South Side, Hilberseimer sought to identify these larger forces. The key question, already apparent in 1950, was to ask if it was possible to control the processes of decay, dilapidation, and demolition in the suddenly outmoded urban core. Even to this day, Hilberseimer's solution to this problem seems ingenious, elegant, and almost effortless in its simplicity. He proposed to literally reproduce and subsequently control the processes of disaggregation by the introduction of a symmetrically formed figure into the disintegrating urban field. This figure, a fragment of the field from which it emerged, would be produced by the very forces that were so largely in play at the time–urban decline and outward dispersion. In other words, the remedy for disaggregation would come from disaggregation conceived as a designed process that played itself out over a specific period of time. The effort, then, would not be to contain urban destruction and stabilize the area through a restoration process, but instead to quicken its demise to the advantage of all that would follow. Responding as an urban designer rather than a sociologist or a planner–form-based rather than data-based–Hilberseimer produced an exquisite series of proposals for Chicago that both explained the dramatic collapse of the street-and-block paradigm and fully anticipated the next stage of the city's expansion. Hilberseimer would call these proposals "Replanning Projects."

PHASE DIAGRAMS

In order to describe Hilberseimer's promotion of disaggregation in the inner city, I will examine a single emblematic project that he published in *The Nature of Cities*.[1] This book was a reorganization of a previous text written in Europe and titled *The New City*.[2] For the latter book, Hilberseimer edited several early projects and added a decade of new work, including his approach to planned disaggregation. In this way, *The Nature of Cities* was not conceived as a response to the problem of the blighted city, but was primarily about the next stage of the city's decentralized and dispersed expansion. The beauty of Hilberseimer's response is that the collapse of the inner city is described as one aspect of a single urban dynamic. The Replanning Projects make clear that the force driving the decline of inner city neighborhoods was the same force that was driving the breakneck expansion to the west of the city.

Although the inclusion of the new Replanning Projects in *The Nature of Cities* may not seem significant, it signaled an important clarification of Hilberseimer's approach to urbanism. As opposed to Wright and Le Corbusier, Hilberseimer did not produce masterplans. From the very beginning, he emphasized the aggregation of the urban "unit" or part rather than composing or masterplanning the whole. While there were aspects of aggregation in the Radiant City and Broadacre, neither of these projects left the overall planning to a simple aggregative process; both architects composed their overall plans. Modern urbanism is in fact so closely tied to overall planning that we tend to think that masterplanning is the equivalent of modern urbanism. Yet, Hilberseimer delivered a version of the modern city as pure aggregation and the differences between the two approaches are worth noting. Encoding the ultimate design of a city into a single unit capable of aggregating and producing multiple outcomes requires an entirely different mindset than composing an exact specification for a city in its entirety and fixing that specification in one final plan. Unlike any of his con-

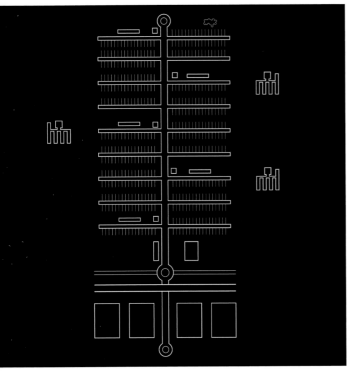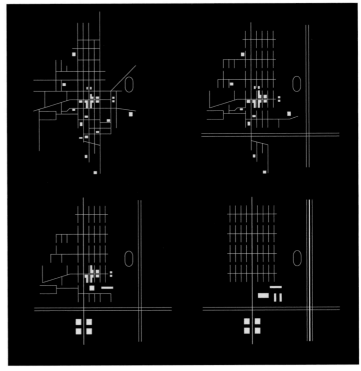

106   LEFT: LUDWIG HILBERSEIMER, "SETTLEMENT UNIT," IN *THE NATURE OF CITIES*, 1955.
RIGHT: LUDWIG HILBERSEIMER, "THE REPLANNING OF ELKHORN, WYOMING," IN *THE NATURE OF CITIES*, 1955.

temporaries, Hilberseimer designed, in 1927, a basic unit of urban reproduction that became the DNA for all his subsequent projects. Called the "Settlement Unit," the symmetrical spine-like form first appeared in *The New City* and was reproduced again in the *The Nature of Cities* as the basis for the new work, including the Replanning Projects. It is not an accident that the spine unit reappears in his inner city proposals, nor is it an accident that these proposals rejected tabula rasa planning. As opposed to, for example, Le Corbusier's *Plan Voisin* (1925), the Replanning Projects reject the demolition and replacement of old cities ex-nihilo in favor of a staged transformation of old into new. While similar to many of the projects that were illustrated in *The New City* (including a reorganization of Chicago), the Replanning Projects are not presented in a single plan. They instead sequence their realization in series of either three or four frames which evolve over an unspecified period of time from frame to frame. In contrast to a tabula rasa approach, the first frame is always an existing grid organization while the final frame is always structured by a series of Hilberseimer's new spine aggregates. The intermediate frames are perhaps the most fascinating–freely interpolated com-binations of the first and final states giving the impression that the number of interpolated states is arbitrary. The result is a series of phase diagrams that track a dynamic, evolutionary process rather than a fixed or final form.

Before examining a specific Replanning Project, one comment on the nature of Hilberseimer's peculiar mode of diagrammatic design is necessary. It has always

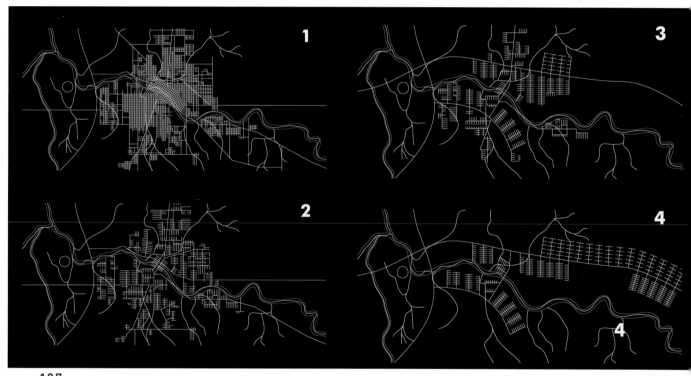

107   LUDWIG HILBERSEIMER, "REPLANNING OF ROCKFORD, ILLINOIS," IN *THE NATURE OF CITIES*, 1955.

been difficult to decide exactly to which genre of drawing Hilberseimer's urban plans belong. In their extreme abstraction they remain enigmatic, raising as many questions as they answer. Are they intended for execution, or are they abstract diagrams? Are they a sequence of demolition plans or merely a thought experiment? Are they utopian projections or are they lucid descriptions of what already exists? Taken as a literal plan of action, the Replanning Projects constitute a dubious strategy–the demolition of valuable urban resources alone begs credibility. Taken as a thought experiment in the nature of contemporary urbanism, however, the phase diagrams are both absurd and daring propositions which, in their abstraction, invite a broad range of interpretation. The most obvious interpretation sees the discrete stages of urban demolition as taking shape over an unspecified period of time. While this reading is obvious enough, it is inconclusive. The sequence of diagrams seem to be describing, not only a demolition schedule, but also something about the inner logic of the grid form itself.

The transition from grid to spine moves between two diametrically opposed states that are nevertheless bound to a single transformative process. This process can be interpreted in at least three ways. One interpretation could be called a *temporal transformation*, in which the historical process of grid fragmentation tracks the evolution of the twentieth-century city from the industrial gridiron at the beginning of the century to the consumer cul-de-sac at the end of it. A second interpretation of the transformative process could be called a *spatial transformation*, which isolates three discrete cross sections through the present-day city from the core to the periphery. (Here, the first diagram stands for the gridded streets of the urban core, the second diagram stands for the superblocks typical to the first ring subdivision surrounding the core, and the third diagram represents the ex-urban cul-de-sac.) A third and perhaps most intriguing interpretation of the transformative process could be termed a *morphological transformation*, in which the stages in the diagram demonstrate the unfolding of an internal self-referencing or autonomous logic, like the spontaneous erosion of an open grid network into a simple symmetrical spine or figure. Far more than a demolition schedule or the key stages of twentieth-century urbanism, the Replanning Projects show an autonomous geometric evolution of the spine out of its gridiron predecessor. These three types of transformation will become apparent with reference to a specific Replanning Project.

TRANSFORMING THE GRIDIRON: MARQUETTE PARK

Of the four Replanning Projects done for Chicago, Hilberseimer's plan for the redevelopment of Marquette Park is the clearest and most emblematic presentation of his urban logic. The project is described by a three-stage diagram that shows a large 840-block redevelopment area defined by continuous gridiron infrastructure and interrupted by a large rectangular urban park along one edge. The park itself was part of a system of fourteen neighborhood parks designed for Chicago in 1903 by the Olmsted Brothers. The 100-block, 323-acre Marquette Park is the largest of the fourteen parks. (While embedded in the neighborhood the site played a large part in the city's history. Serving an all-white constituency, it was, for example, the site of an important civil rights protest in 1966 led by Martin Luther King). The park itself straddles the boundary of the 13th, 15th, and 18th Wards of Chicago with each of these wards benefiting from its open space. Hilberseimer's Replanning Project effectively splits these three wards apart, eliminating the overlap; in the process, it expanded the park's open space approximately sevenfold. In a remarkable demonstration of planned disaggregation, the project transforms the neighborhood from a single, large gridiron district organized around a framed space into six separate cul-de-sac spines, which float in an entirely new, modernist conception of urban space.

In the first stage of the project, the existing gridiron constructs park space within a frame of surrounding blocks from which that space is subtracted. Despite the fact that it is large and green, it is traditionally formed urban space that gives focus to the larger urban grid that otherwise extends in all directions. In its existing configuration, the streets are continuous and open and the park space is framed and closed. There are ninety-five street entrances to Marquette Park and the district as a whole contains 812 intersections, most of which are open, four-way intersections. The second stage of the Replanning Project is the one transitional stage, and it negotiates a compromise between the open street configuration of the existing neighborhood and the closed, cul-de-sac configuration of the final stage. However, this configuration is more than a provisional intermediate stage and is instead a mode of urbanization in itself. In this configuration there are thirty-three street entrances to the project area. Despite the fact that the surface area of the streets remains largely intact, this stage completely reorganizes the territory; in the second stage the project area contains only half the

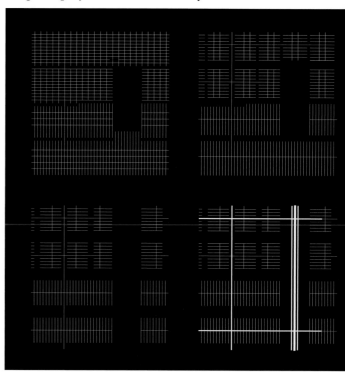

LUDWIG HILBERSEIMER, "THE REPLANNING OF MARQUETTE PARK, CHICAGO, ILLINOIS," IN *THE NATURE OF CITIES*, 1955.

number of original street intersections: 438. The final state of the project shows the collapse of the frame that defined the original bounded park and the emergence of a new, unbounded spatial network. No longer a discrete urban park, the remaining residential streets now float in a space of an entirely different order and magnitude than that of a traditional park. Inverting the original pattern, the streets are now figurative or closed spines and the space is continuous or open, less a park, more of a parkway. The final frame reveals a paradox: a discontinuity or closure of urban form (continuous street grid) produces a continuity or openness of unbounded urban space. In the final stage of the project, there are just seven street entrances to Marquette Park and the district retains only 360 intersections of the original 812.

As streets and intersections are demolished, the grid grows coarser, and the street continuity breaks down as the amount of open space explodes. What emerges from this process is a series of large-scale, spine-based figures, variations of the Settlement Unit that Hilberseimer employed in his projects since 1927. The Marquette Park project is, indeed, something of an original sketch of the Settlement Unit where the DNA of the new city is shown to evolve out of the old. Yet while the spine evolves out of the gridiron streets, it does more than simply modify the road surface. In this regard, the spine replaces the urban block as a unit of urban aggregation. In Hilberseimer's project, as in the Megalopolis it imitated, block-by-block would be replaced by spine-by-spine, both within and without the city. As the figures emerged in response to

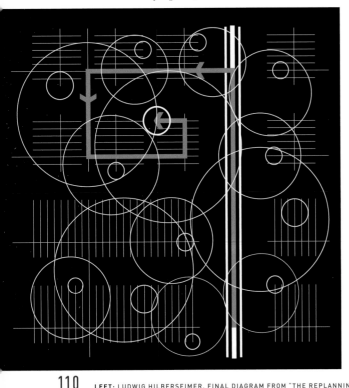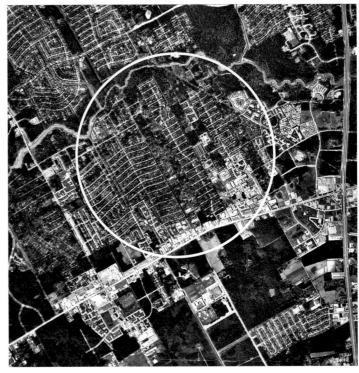

110   **LEFT:** LUDWIG HILBERSEIMER, FINAL DIAGRAM FROM "THE REPLANNING OF MARQUETTE PARK, CHICAGO, ILLINOIS," IN *THE NATURE OF CITIES*, 1955 AND OVERLAY WITH CIRCULATION ROUTE AND SETTLEMENT OVERLAPS. **RIGHT:** AERIAL VIEW OF THE AREA AROUND FARM AND MARKET ROADS IN HOUSTON, 1960. THE MORPHOLOGICAL DNA OF MEGALOPOLIS — THE SPINE FORM DISCOVERED BY HILBERSEIMER — IS INSTANTLY RECOGNIZABLE IN VIRTUALLY ANY STREET PATTERN CONSTRUCTED AFTER 1950.

redevelopment and the explosive growth at the periphery, a new unity would emerge, tying inner city redevelopment to the new peripheral spines of cul-de-sac urbanism.

CONCLUSION

Like the grid form from which it came, the spine possesses the simple, internal logic capable of structuring infinitely complex urban environments. For centuries, the grid strictly regulated the form of the city. Uncontested, street-and-block urbanism possessed the authority, if not the inevitability, of natural law. What is at stake in such authority is the ability to define an autonomous urban culture capable of trumping political, economic, cultural contingencies in favor of highly valued urban qualities, including public space. While today this kind of authority seems like a pipe dream, its existence in the pre-modern grid forms of our urban cores, like Chicago, is proof enough of its possibility. Indeed, it is this possibility that constitutes our very definition of urbanism despite the fact that gridiron urbanism was superseded over a half-century ago.

The time of the gridded city has past, but the idea of an autonomous urban logic has not. The spine, like the grid, supports a complexity that grows out of simple pattern. Hilberseimer's urban project suggests that a typical form for sprawl is not only possible, it already exists. The simplest form of the cul-de-sac – the cross-axial spine – was first recognized by Hilberseimer in 1927, but it has gone unrecognized for the role it plays in contemporary urban development. It remains in the shadow of outmoded forms of street-and-block urbanism against which it is routinely defined as suburban. What the abstract readings of Hilberseimer's diagrammatic projects reveal is the transformation of twentieth-century urban form at its most basic level. The transition from block to spine, however, is more than just a substitution of one form for another. If the aggregate unit of contemporary urban development is understood to seamlessly evolve out of urban history, then that history – all of it – is at our disposal. What this grants designers is access to the properties of traditional cities that have long been lost to modern urbanism. More important, however, is that it provides a template for the necessary transformation of these forms. The implications of this unity of logic unfolding across the urbanism of the twentieth century are significant. Form bridges the post-war divide between core and periphery, inner city and suburb, Metropolis and Megalopolis, structure and sprawl and, for the first time, allows us to see and operate on Chicago as a single entity.

The work of Hilberseimer made the new realities of the post-war city legible. The divide of twenty-five/seventy-five percent that defines Chicago today has been replaced, at least conceptually, with Hilberseimer's new unity, based on an aggregation of spine forms. The old urban/suburban divide is replaced, not by a masterplan but by a new aggregate urbanism that is uncannily similar to what exists in the Megalopolis today. For the aggregation of spines not only describes Hilberseimer's project, it also describes the urban expansion that has taken place around the globe for the past half-century. What Hilberseimer accomplished is to make the neglected seventy-five percent of Chicagoland legible and operable and of a piece with the gridiron that came before it. The tools needed to create this understanding were born in Chicago at precisely the moment that the great tide of population growth turned away from the traditional form of street-and-block urbanism. Out of the malaise of a brutal, inner-city transformation, a new, unified urban model was proposed. Had that model been better understood, it would have had the value of making all parts of the city equally important, not just the older and more familiar ones. And we would not be left clinging to the diminishing significance of the grid form, our ability to affect change gradually dwindling to zero.

NOTES

[1] Ludwig Hilberseimer, *The Nature of Cities, Origin, Growth, and Decline; Pattern and Form; Planning Problems* (Chicago: Paul Theobald, 1955).

[2] Ludwig Hilbersheimer, *The New City: Principles of Planning* (Chicago: Paul Theobald, 1944).

MIRKO ZARDINI

FOLDING BEFORE DIGITAL

In the winter of 1992, while teaching at the University of Illinois at Chicago (UIC), Greg Lynn was invited by Stanley Tigerman to participate in *Architexturally Speaking*. The exhibition presented the work of ten UIC faculty members, who were invited to choose and re-work an existing Chicago building.

In retrospect, the Sears Tower was an almost inevitable choice for Lynn. After having explored for years – while working with Peter Eisenman and by himself – the modification of geometrical modules in both plan and space, the Sears Tower, with its structure of nine bundled tubes, must have seemed like the perfect case study. Rejecting the traditional idea of vertical office buildings, Lynn laid his project horizontally in a strand of land adjacent to the existing Sears Tower. At the same time, he transformed the structure into a system of deformed fibers and filaments, creating a complex building balanced between its internal order and the external forces of the context.

Lynn hand-drew the project – using adjustable triangles, compasses, and rubber spline curves – in eight weeks of intense, almost reclusive work. It was an extreme exercise, and his last, in experimenting with the possibilities offered by traditional tools to represent his architectural vision. One year later, in 1993, Lynn edited the issue of *Architectural Design* called "Folding in Architecture," where the Stranded Sears Tower project was presented together with works of, among others, Peter Eisenman, Chuck Hoberman, Frank Gehry, and Shoei Yoh. Interestingly, none of the projects presented in this issue "took recourse to digital visualization and mapping as an explanation of their shape and form."

THICK THIN

SARAH WHITING

114

OMA's McCormick Tribune Campus Center at the Illinois Institute of Technology replaces the material thinness of minimalism with an architecture of fattened flatness. It does so not by aspiring to Mies's *almost-nothingness*, but by multiplying *somethingness*. Chicago is flat. But at the McCormick Center, flat is thick. This building, whose design conceit depends entirely on plan, is knowable only through section. Its single story holds together many levels. Sectional depth is further accentuated by transverse experience: the axial is replaced by the diagonal, which means that everything is viewed on the oblique, offering depth of field rather than the singularity of the axial one-point perspective.

Straight-up, vertical surfaces are where the building offers its most direct challenge to minimalist immateriality. Glass sheds aspirations to non-dimensional transparency or two-dimensional imagery: honeycombed Panelite is embedded within a double-glazed system, making air itself substantial. When the afternoon sun hits the orange Panelite of the building's zigzagging primary façade, the spaces behind it become a single, massive orange swath – an interiorized sunset fog.

Surprisingly, saturation does not result in chaos. The verticals of the McCormick Center fade in and fade out, accumulating without competing. Lenticular wallpaper makes the flat walls almost fuzzy. Hundreds of two-and-a-half-inch-high black-and-white icons – new "universal" figures denoting tasks like computing, sleeping, music, and even romance – crowd together to form larger icons, via a pixilated pointillism. On one long wall their dot matrix offers an IIT history lesson, illustrating the institution's founding fathers. The most clever, most unsettling portrait is that of the fully mature, slightly dour Mies, whose head, split horizontally into an orange/white top and clear/white bottom, constitutes the building's front door; *Being John Malkovitch* merges with Samuel Beckett's *The Unnamable:* "an outside and an inside and me in the middle, perhaps that's what I am."

Irreverent? Yes, maybe, although a sixteen-foot-high portrait facing a major thoroughfare is also an honor to which no other architect can lay claim.

AMERICAN MODERN

THE CHICAGO SCHOOL AND THE INTERNATIONAL STYLE AT NEW YORK'S MUSEUM OF MODERN ART

JOANNA MERWOOD-SALISBURY

The idea of a "Chicago School" of architecture has assumed the mantle of modern "mythology" in the sense described by Roland Barthes, a historical construction whose ideological origins have been lost or deliberately forgotten. A signifier of American dominance in both technological and aesthetic innovation, it rests on the implicit understanding that architectural modernism has a strong foundation in the built products of capitalist urbanism. Architectural historians have begun to interrogate this mythology, examining when, how, and why it was constructed, as well as the role it continues to play in our image of Chicago and other global cities.[1] This essay focuses on the role played by New York's Museum of Modern Art (MoMA) in creating and disseminating the idea of the Chicago School of architecture to its influential audience during the 1930s. As I will show, the museum's promotion of a group of buildings and architects categorized under the heading Chicago School was influenced by the writing of avant-garde architects and critics in Europe, and was closely tied to parallel efforts to promote the so-called "International Style," a depoliticized version of the modern style beginning to appear in Germany, France, and the Netherlands. Starting with a modest exhibition, *Early Modern Architecture: Chicago 1870–1910*, curated in 1933 by Henry-Russell Hitchcock and Philip Johnson, MoMA positioned the early Chicago skyscraper as a formal object worthy of aesthetic consideration; not just an innovative and sophisticated technological object, but one of the nation's greatest artistic achievements. Throughout the 1930s and 1940s the museum mounted further exhibitions and employed increasingly sophisticated media, including publications, radio, and even film, to promote what it saw as formal parallels between the tall office buildings of late-nineteenth-century Chicago and the International Style. The primary goal of these efforts was to "naturalize" the International Style for the United States by providing it with American origins, linking it to capitalism rather than socialist movements in Europe, and by arguing that its representative architectural type was not social housing but the skyscraper.

Hitchcock and Johnson's aim in linking Chicago to the International Style was intended to "correct" not only the American perception of the modern style, its political symbolism and geographical origins, but also the course of contemporary building in the US. *Early Modern Architecture: Chicago* was conceived at a time when the skyscraper was under threat as a sustainable type. In 1933 utopian visions for future skyscraper cities were disintegrating in the wake of the global financial collapse of 1929. In this context, the exhibition acted as a form of "operative history," an instrumental use of the past in order to promote action in the present.[2] The curators used the temporary halt in building production caused by the Great Depression as an opportunity to criticize the products of the 1920s boom – the fashionable setback skyscraper with Art Deco massing and ornamental motifs – and at the same time they suggested an American precedent for future building. Co-opting European interest in the simplicity and apparent structural expressionism of the first tall office buildings erected in Chicago, they convinced their audience that the skyscraper was an important part of both its cultural heritage and its urban future.

POSITIONING THE CHICAGO SKYSCRAPER
AS THE TRUE MODERN AMERICAN ARCHITECTURE

In the spring of 1932 the historian Henry-Russell Hitchcock and the critic Philip Johnson introduced America to a movement they called the International Style in a landmark show at the Museum of Modern Art in New York. During 1930 and 1931 they had traveled throughout Europe, accompanied by the museum's director Alfred H. Barr Jr., touring recent building projects as well as exhibitions of contemporary architecture and design. Influenced by what they had seen, their exhibition, *Modern Architecture: International Exhibition* (often called the "International Style" show) became the most famous architecture show ever mounted in the US, perhaps in the world, one with an enduring impact. But that influence would come later. This essay is concerned with the immediate future: it is about what happened next. In the summer of 1932, after the International Style exhibition had been demounted, Hitchcock and Johnson traveled to Chicago in search of local sources for the International Style, sources that pre-dated

118   INSTALLATION VIEWS OF *MODERN ARCHITECTURE: INTERNATIONAL EXHIBITION* AT THE MUSEUM OF MODERN ART, NEW YORK, 1932.

and perhaps influenced its appearance in Europe.[3] The material they gathered became the basis for MoMA's second architecture exhibition, *Early Modern Architecture: Chicago 1870–1910*, displayed in January and February of 1933.

While the *International Style* show has had obvious lasting influence, popularizing a particular style of modern building, as well as generating an ongoing debate about the relationship between aesthetics and politics, the follow-up has left few obvious traces.[4] The museum's archives contain no installation photographs and only two publicity images of it, both showing Philip Johnson posing with models illustrating the transition from masonry construction to steel-framing. Unlike the earlier exhibition, there was no printed catalogue, only a mimeographed typescript. The lack of photographs depicting *Early Modern Architecture: Chicago* indicates that Johnson most likely did not employ the dynamic installation techniques, such as floating panels and scrim ceilings with hidden lighting, that he had admired during his visits to Germany, and which he later successfully exploited in his *Machine Art* exhibition of 1934.[5] If he had, then surely photographs would have been taken. Much more modest, this exhibition consisted of thirty-three large format (24 x 30 inch) photographs mounted without frames on basswood, along with three models, and some wall texts. It featured many buildings that have since become familiar icons including the Leiter, Home Insurance, Tacoma, Monadnock, and Reliance Buildings. While the majority of the subjects were tall office buildings constructed in the down-

119 LEFT: INSTALLATION VIEW OF *MACHINE ART* AT THE MUSEUM OF MODERN ART, NEW YORK, 1934.
RIGHT: WILLIAM LE BARON JENNEY, FIRST LEITER BUILDING, CHICAGO, 1879.

town Loop before 1900, the curators included some residential and institutional buildings, including Frank Lloyd Wright's Winslow House (1893) and Dwight Perkins' Carl Schurz High School (1908). Together they were meant to illustrate, as the press release claimed, "the most important creative period in American architecture which saw the birth of the skyscraper and a new type of modern design suitable to it."[6]

Hitchcock and Johnson's goal was to convince their viewers that Chicago architects had managed to transform the raw industrial power and commercial drive that characterized that city into something beautiful and unprecedented in the field of art history. That transformation was reinforced by wall texts setting out two chronologies, one on the "Technical Development of the Skyscraper" and the other on its "Aesthetic Development." These texts argued that the aesthetic development of the skyscraper was secondary to, but directly derived from, the invention of the steel-frame. The three models on display, illustrating "The All-Masonry Building," "The Masonry Building with Steel Skeleton," and "The Steel Skeleton Building," dramatized this structural evolution. The story of this evolution was privileged for one reason in particular: the aesthetic possibility of ever-more transparent curtain-walls.

The curators' emphasis on the aesthetics of the steel-frame was based in their desire to draw a direct link between the formal characteristics of the early Chicago skyscraper and those of the International Style. In his introduction to the International

120 LEFT: D. H. BURNHAM AND CO., RELIANCE BUILDING, CHICAGO, 1895.
RIGHT: DETAIL OF ORNAMENTED TERRACOTTA TILE, RELIANCE BUILDING.

Style catalogue, Barr defined these characteristics as an emphasis on volume as opposed to mass, and on the "intrinsic elegance of materials" rather than "applied ornament."[7] Although Chicago architects of the 1880s and 1890s (Louis Sullivan in particular) had engaged in a series of complex aesthetic experiments to re-imagine ornament for the industrial era, Hitchcock and Johnson preferred to present the ornament on Chicago School buildings as conceptually non-existent, concentrating instead on the simple forms underneath.[8]

The erasure of ornament from the early Chicago skyscrapers was in support of one of the exhibition's secondary agendas: a critique of the Art Deco skyscrapers for which New York City was becoming famous. Only a few years earlier Barr had dismissed the skyscraper as "the architectural taste of real estate speculators, renting agents and mortgage brokers!"[9] The only New York City example included in the exhibition, George Post's World Building of 1890, was a negative one, intended to demonstrate the failure of New York architects to grasp the aesthetic significance of new building technologies. Johnson argued that contemporary Manhattan skyscrapers were the result of New York architects' continued dependence on ornament, that the Art Deco megaliths lining Park and Madison Avenues were a false and inauthentic form of the new style, "modernistic" rather than "modern."[10] (The specific example he cited was Arthur Loomis Harmon's Shelton Hotel of 1924.) In Chicago, Hitchcock and Johnson found products of commercial development they could place in opposition to these examples of nineteenth and early-twentieth-century eclecticism. *Early Mod-*

121 LEFT: GEORGE POST, WORLD BUILDING, PARK ROW, NEW YORK, 1890.
RIGHT: ARTHUR LOOMIS HARMON, SHELTON HOTEL, NEW YORK, 1924.

ern Architecture: Chicago posited the existence of a "Chicago formula" of skyscraper design based on structural expression that, even when banal, was superior to the revivalism and capricious stylistic invention characteristic of New York City skyscrapers.

Beyond this comparison between the two economic centers of the US, the exhibition allowed its curators to challenge the prevailing belief that modern architecture was a European invention exercised primarily in socialist countries in the form of public housing and institutional buildings. Instead, the curators suggested, the International Style had an equally important antecedent in a type created within the framework of commercial financing, speculative development, and private ownership.

THE CHICAGO SCHOOL AS PRECURSOR TO THE INTERNATIONAL STYLE

Why was it was necessary to link Chicago to the International Style? MoMA's formalist approach to architecture was designed to deflect ambivalence about the ideological message of modern design. The politics of the modern style was a topic of debate not only in the US, but also internationally. Late in 1932 the National Socialist party of Germany forced the closure of the Bauhaus in Dessau. Early in 1933 plans for the fourth CIAM Congress in Moscow were abandoned under pressure from the Soviets, and the event was hurriedly relocated to a cruise ship in the Mediterranean.[11] Although the reaction was less extreme in the US, modern design was widely perceived as foreign and potentially dangerous because of its basis in socialism.[12] In promoting the International Style, MoMA found it necessary to advertise it as thoroughly native and democratic in its origins.

Although *Early Modern Architecture: Chicago* was an exhibition of American buildings curated by Americans, its staging was largely prompted by a European view of its subject. It was one of the first popular presentations in the US of the kind of paean to American commercial and industrial buildings first expressed by avant-garde architects and critics such as Ludwig Hilberseimer, Erich Mendelsohn, Bruno Taut, Walter Behrendt, and Richard Neutra.[13] Various books by these Europeans presented commercial architecture in New York and Chicago, the product of rapid capitalist expansion, as an anonymous and objective vernacular, evidence of the potential of industrialized building techniques for social liberation. By the early 1930s American architects and critics including Lewis Mumford and Hitchcock had begun to represent this version of architectural history to Americans in a significantly amended form.[14] First they transformed the European view of early Chicago skyscrapers as basically authorless products of industrialization into objects of conscious design. But while Mumford held on to the potential of modern architecture for social emancipation, Hitchcock preferred to concentrate on its formal aspects, playing down its political context.

Hitchcock presented the early Chicago skyscraper not as the vernacular product of the industrial age, but as the artistic creation of a group of named individuals, a category that could be considered a "school" in the art-historical tradition. *Early Modern Architecture: Chicago* was a tool for communicating the idea that Chicago architects working in the 1880s and 1890s represented a unified "school," one that created a unified and innovative aesthetic response to new construction technologies and building programs. As Nina Stritzler-Levine has shown, Hitchcock saw the medium of the exhibition as a legitimate scholarly enterprise, an important tool for the communication of academic ideas: "As an architectural historian and curator Hitchcock adhered to a diachronic reading of modern architecture. He established genealogies of master architects, privileged so-called great monuments, and presented history as a linear progression of styles."[15] As a completely new building type, he believed the skyscraper occupied an important role in this progression: It was the form through which the modern style found its most current realization.

While they acknowledged the "authors" of the Chicago skyscraper – William Le Baron Jenney, Daniel H. Burnham, John W. Root, and Louis Sullivan – Hitchcock and Johnson focused on the skyscraper as an autonomous technical object at the expense of its urban and social context. As contemporary scholars have discussed, the appearance of the tall office building was not due solely to the invention of the steel-frame, but also to new economic practices, specifically the financial entity of the corporation, speculative ventures by large groups of individual investors grouped together in syndicates.[16] By including biographical information about architects but no information about the location of these buildings, the men who commissioned them, or the economic circumstances of their development, the curators presented the Chicago skyscraper in the same manner as a work of fine art. MoMA's patrons had made their money from business. Now the skyscraper, the product of business and previously viewed in terms of economic value, could be presented at a museum of modern art in the company of the country's finest aesthetic productions.

Where European architects had co-opted Chicago as an early and imperfect test site for future skyscraper cities situated in radically altered socio-political landscapes, MoMA employed Chicago's commercial architecture for quite a different purpose, as a series of beautiful objects testifying to the success of capitalism. With this exhibition, the museum helped naturalize, as Barthes would say, an ideological view of the early American skyscraper, a view embedded in the mythology of the Chicago School of architecture.

PUBLICIZING THE CHICAGO SCHOOL OF ARCHITECTURE MYTHOLOGY

During the remainder of the 1930s and into the early 1940s MoMA continued to promote the idea of the Chicago School of architecture as a native precursor to the International Style. Where Johnson focused on more contemporary subjects during the brief time he remained at the museum, Hitchcock continued to look backwards, locating precursors to the modern aesthetic in mid-nineteenth-century America. In the spring of 1933 Johnson curated *Work of Young Architects of the Middle West*, which showcased Midwestern architects, including Fred Keck, Howard T. Fisher (whose "General House" system of prefabricated housing was featured), and Hamilton Beatty (who had worked in Le Corbusier's office), all of whom worked in what could be considered the International Style. He called this show the "logical successor to the International Exhibition."[17]

Meanwhile Hitchcock kept looking to the past for clues to the future. His next project was an exhibition and a book on Boston architect H. H. Richardson. Organized with the help of Johnson before he left MoMA, *Architecture by H. H. Richardson* went on display in early 1936. This exhibition advanced Hitchcock's claim that Richardson was the source of American modernism. It abandoned the structural determinism evident in *Early Modern Architecture: Chicago*, and argued instead that the modern style in the US was not the result of the pragmatic appropriation of new technologies, particularly the steel-frame, but a deliberate formal sensibility dating back to the mid-nineteenth century. Hitchcock revised the popular view of Richardson's influence, de-emphasizing the significance of the Richardsonian Romanesque, and arguing instead that his work was valuable because it emphasized pure form and composition, that is, that it represented a proto-modern aesthetic. Overcoming critical and scholarly

123

ambivalence about his florid ornament, Hitchcock named Sullivan as the immediate heir to Richardson's artistry. Finally, Hitchcock diverged from Johnson by identifying Frank Lloyd Wright, rather than Keck, Fisher, or Beatty, as the most relevant contemporary descendent of the Chicago School.[18]

Populated with a pantheon of heroes, the mythology of the Chicago School was now complete: prompted by the example of Richardson, Sullivan had produced the highest achievement of modern architecture in America, the skyscraper. Wright had translated this modernist sensibility into domestic design in the early twentieth century and promoted it across the Atlantic where it spurred a new generation of modernists. Throughout the 1930s MoMA continued to repeat this genealogy in a series of exhibitions and multi-media productions. In 1934 the museum's publicity director Sarah Newmeyer, organized, with the backing of the Carnegie Corporation, a series of radio programs broadcast under the title "Art in America" on the local NBC station on Saturday nights. Intended to promote the idea that modern art and design had been a long-standing national endeavor, it was supported by illustrated mail order supplements including essays on architecture written by Hitchcock, Johnson, and Catherine Bauer. In this way the museum's message about the Chicago School was delivered directly into American homes via radio waves and postal communication.[19] In 1938 MoMA produced a forty-minute film, "Evolution of the Skyscraper," written by the new curator of the architecture department, John McAndrew, and directed by E. Francis Thompson.[20] This film was incorporated into an exhibition entitled *Three Centuries of American Architecture*, which circulated to a dozen venues including other museums and academic institutions as well as department stores between 1939 and 1941. In 1946 it was sent to Great Britain under the auspices of the Office of War Information as part of the United States government's propaganda activities during World War II. [21]

"Evolution of the Skyscraper" employed the accessible and popular medium of the film to link early Chicago architecture with urban projects in the present day. It began with the Chicago School and concluded with heroic images of utopian skyscraper cities by Le Corbusier and Richard Neutra. Still photographs were interspersed with graphic diagrams and panning shots of Chicago and New York. Title cards displayed hyperbolic prose: the steel-frame was "the greatest revolution in architectural construction since the Gothic system six hundred and fifty years before." Where *Early Modern Architecture: Chicago* illustrated the tectonic transformation from masonry to the steel-frame with models, the film used images of crustacean and vertebrate biological structures superimposed over images of the same buildings. The film also made

explicit MoMA's intent to employ history to influence the future, voicing approval of contemporary skyscrapers without historicist or overtly art deco trappings, including Raymond Hood's Daily News and McGraw Hill Buildings, Associated Architect's Rockefeller Center, and Howe and Lescaze's PSFS Building in Philadelphia, all presented as legitimate descendents of the Chicago School. In the process, the central message of *Early Modern Architecture: Chicago* was telegraphed and exaggerated into a popular mythology in which Chicago became the origin of the future of the modern city.

OPERATIVE HISTORY:
THE CHICAGO SCHOOL AND THE CONTEMPORARY BUILDING SITUATION

The mythology of the Chicago School of architecture must be seen in relation to the dramatic reshaping of American cities and the American building industry caused by capitalist cycles of boom and bust, especially the Great Depression. Hitchcock and Johnson's display of a select group of early Chicago skyscrapers as forerunners of the International Style was not a disinterested historical exercise. It was a form of operative history; a presentation of the past intended to influence building in the present. Their championing of the work of Jenney, Burnham & Root, Sullivan, and Wright, came at a critical time in the short life of the skyscraper type. After a period of what economists describe as "overbuilding" or "overinvestment" in commercial building stock during the 1920s, skyscrapers were increasingly losing their value and many of the early tall commercial buildings, now almost forty years old, were being demolished and replaced by low buildings or even vacant lots used for parking.[22] As some contemporary review-

125 RAYMOND HOOD, MCGRAW HILL BUILDING, NEW YORK, 1931, FROM THE EXHIBITION ALBUM *MODERN ARCHITECTURE: INTERNATIONAL EXHIBITION*. ALTHOUGH THE MCGRAW HILL BUILDING SHARES THE SAME STEPPED-BACK PROFILE AS THE SHELTON HOTEL, ITS CURTAIN-WALL IS EXPOSED BY LARGE HORIZONTAL WINDOWS AND IT LACKS HISTORICIZING ORNAMENT AT THE ROOF LINE, FORMALLY LINKING IT WITH THE INTERNATIONAL STYLE.

ers noted, the argument that early Chicago skyscrapers were valuable artistic productions was particularly significant at a time when many of the first generation of Chicago office buildings, including the Home Insurance Building, were being demolished because they were no longer economically viable. "The museum's exhibition will [...]

be the first record of a great architecture which is vanishing under the sledgehammer of the housewrecker," claimed the *Brooklyn Daily Eagle*.[23] This process was exacerbated by the stock market crash of 1929. Planning for new commercial construction had virtually ceased and it would take almost thirty years for American cities to recover. At the same time that the skyscraper was becoming less financially viable, a growing trend toward urban decentralization suggested that the building type might become obsolete altogether.

Along with their European counterparts, by the early 1930s American urban planners and social reformers were beginning to think that the densely built, vertical cities that had appeared in the early twentieth century were inherently uneconomic, inefficient, and unhealthy. In 1942 an economist summarized the problems of the American city as: "poverty and inequality, dirt, smoke, and waste, noise and strain, delinquency and crime, exploitation of urban land, slums and blighted areas, housing difficulties, obsolescence, dislocation of industry, urban transit, lag in public improvements, legal obstructions, and tax tangles."[24] In response, architects tried to rationalize the urban landscape, focusing on the introduction of zoning legislation to restrict building size and function, along with hierarchies of transportation, and more open, green spaces.[25] These new zoning regulations worked in concert with new communication and transportation technologies to decentralize American cities. If the skyscraper was to survive, then a new rationale had to be found for its continued existence, one based in aesthetics rather than economics. Although the skyscraper had ceased to be, at least temporarily, a profitable economic unit in the American city, it still held incalculable value as a signifier of American power. By the early 1930s it had become the symbolic image rather than literal product of capitalism. This was the agenda behind *Early Modern Architecture: Chicago*, namely to present the skyscraper as the original and essential modern building type, one that could not be so easily abandoned. This rhetorical strategy was remarkably effective in influencing the rebuilding of American and other global cities after World War II.[26]

In 1932 MoMA introduced Americans to a cohesive and depoliticized version of modern architecture it called the International Style. In 1933 it created a backwards chronology for that style, transporting it in space and time to the middle of America, situating the first skyscrapers built in Chicago as its earliest embodiment. Throughout the 1930s and into the 1940s MoMA continued to identify Chicago as the home of modern architecture in the US. In doing so, it employed sophisticated mechanisms of publicity including exhibitions, radio, and film to transform an academic narrative into a popular mythology. The mythology of the Chicago

School of architecture claimed the tall office buildings lining the streets of the downtown Loop as primary artifacts in the history of the modern city, the natural result of the positive and progressive technologies of capitalism, as important to the history of modern architecture as the mass housing and institutional buildings constructed under socialist governments in Europe. It also helped ensure that the modern style of skyscraper design, standing apart from its urban context, prismatic and devoid of conventional ornament, became a privileged component of strategies of post-war urban renewal across the US and Europe, a symbol of modernity throughout the world.

NOTES

Earlier versions of this essay were presented as lectures at the Society of Architectural Historians Annual Conference and at the Buell Conference on the History of Architecture at the Temple Hoyne Buell Center for the Study of American Architecture at Columbia University, both in 2010. I am grateful to the editors of this volume, as well as to Barry Bergdoll, Benjamin Flowers, John Harwood, Reinhold Martin, and Claire Zimmerman, for their comments and suggestions.

[1] John Zukowsky, "Introduction to Internationalism in Chicago Architecture," in John Zukowsky, ed., *Chicago Architecture 1872-1922* (New York: Prestel and the Art Institute of Chicago, 1987); Robert Bruegmann, "The Marquette Building and the Myth of the Chicago School," *Threshold*, 5/6 (fall 1991), pp. 7-18, reprinted as "The Myth of the Chicago School," in Charles Waldheim and Katerina Ruedi Ray, eds., *Chicago Architecture: Histories, Revisions, Alternatives* (Chicago: University of Chicago Press, 2005), pp. 15-29; Daniel Bluestone, "Preservation and Renewal in Post-World War II Chicago," *Journal of Architectural Education*, vol. 47, no. 4 (May 1994), pp. 210-223.

[2] Manfredo Tafuri discusses the meaning of "operative criticism" in *Theories and History of Architecture*, trans. Giorgio Verrecchia (London: Granada, 1980). Originally published as *Teorie e storia dell'architettura* (1968).

[3] Chicago architect and ex-Burnham & Root employee Thomas Tallmadge was the local source for much of Hitchcock and Johnson's information about Chicago architecture. Tallmadge's most lasting legacy is the popular belief that William Le Baron Jenney's Home Insurance Building was the "first" skyscraper. Thomas Tallmadge, "Was the Home Insurance Building in Chicago the First Skyscraper of Skeleton Construction?" *Architectural Record*, vol. 76, no. 2 (August 1934), pp. 113-118.

[4] On the impact of the International Style show, see Terence Riley, *International Style: Exhibition 15 and The Museum of Modern Art* (New York: Rizzoli, 1992); and Henry Matthews, "The Promotion of Modern Architecture by the Museum of Modern Art in the 1930s," *Journal of Design History*, vol. 7, no. 1 (1994), pp. 43-59.

[5] Philip Johnson, "The Berlin Building Exposition of 1931," *T-Square*, vol. 2, no. 1, p. 37; Mary Anne Staniszewski, *The Power of Display: A History of Exhibition Installations at the Museum of Modern Art* (Cambridge, MA: MIT Press, 1998), pp. 21, 36-38, 64, 152-160. On Johnson's career as a curator and exhibition designer, see Franz Schulze, *Philip Johnson. Life and Work* (New York: Alfred A. Knopf, 1994), pp. 48-101; Terence Riley, "Portrait of the Curator as a Young Man," in *Philip Johnson and the Museum of Modern Art: Studies in Modern Art no. 6* (New York: Museum of Modern Art and Harry N. Abrams, 1998), pp. 34-69; and Terence Riley and Joshua Sacks, "Philip Johnson: Act One, Scene One - The Museum of Modern Art?," in Emmanuel Petit, ed., *Philip Johnson. The Constancy of Change* (New Haven: Yale University Press, 2009), pp. 60-67.

[6] Press release for *Early Modern Architecture: Chicago 1870-1910* (January 15, 1932). Department of Circulating Exhibitions Records [Folder]. Series II.1.53.1. Museum of Modern Art Archives.

[7] Henry-Russell Hitchcock and Philip Johnson, *The International Style: Architecture Since 1922*, Foreword by Alfred Barr Jr. (New York: W. W. Norton and Company, 1932), p. 29.

[8] On the newly imagined ornament invented for the early Chicago skyscrapers, see Daniel Bluestone, *Constructing Chicago* (Yale University Press: New Haven and London, 1991); and David Van Zanten, *Sullivan's City: The Meaning of Ornament for Louis Sullivan* (New York: W. W. Norton and Co., 2000). On the modernist reading of Chicago School buildings as "unornamented," see Juan Pablo Bonta, *Architecture and its Interpretation: A Study of Expressive Systems in Architecture* (New York: Rizzoli, 1979),

pp. 91-129; and Mark Wigley, *White Walls, Designer Dresses. The Fashioning of Modern Architecture* (Cambridge, MA: MIT Press, 1995), pp. 60-63, 123-125.

[9] Alfred H. Barr, Jr., Foreword, *The International Style*, p. 30.

[10] Philip Johnson, "Skyscraper School of Modern Architecture," *Arts*, vol. 27, no. 8 (May 1931), p. 575.

[11] Eric Mumford, *The CIAM Discourse on Urbanism, 1928-1960* (Cambridge, MA: MIT Press, 2002), pp. 73-74.

[12] Karen Koehler discusses the association often made between modern art and architecture and socialism in American popular culture during the 1920s and 1930s in "The Bauhaus 1919-1928: Gropius in Exile and the Museum of Modern Art," in Richard Etlin, ed., *Art, Culture and Media Under the Third Reich* (Chicago: University of Chicago Press, 2002), pp. 287-315.

[13] Reyner Banham, *The Concrete Atlantis: US Industrial Building and European Modern Architecture* (Cambridge, MA: MIT Press, 1986); and Jean-Louis Cohen, *Scenes of the World to Come: European Architecture and the American Challenge 1893-1960* (Paris/Montreal: Flammarion/Canadian Centre for Architecture, 1995).

[14] Lewis Mumford commented on the fascination avant-garde European architects held for American industrial and commercial buildings in "New York vs. Chicago in Architecture," *Architecture*, 56 (November 1927), pp. 241-244. See also Henry-Russell Hitchcock, *Modern Architecture: Romanticism and Reintegration* (New York: Payson and Clarke, 1929).

[15] Nina Stritzler-Levine, "Curating History, Exhibiting Ideas: Henry-Russell Hitchcock and Architectural Exhibition Practice at the MoMA," in Frank Salmon, ed., *Summerson and Hitchcock: Centenary Essays on Architectural Historiography* (Yale University Press: New Haven and London, 2006), pp. 34-35.

[16] Miles Berger, *They Built Chicago: Entrepreneurs Who Shaped a Great City's Architecture* (Chicago: Bonus Books, 1992); and Carol Willis, *Form Follows Finance: Skyscrapers and Skylines in New York and Chicago* (New York: Princeton Architectural Press, 1995). I explore the social and economic context of the early Chicago skyscraper in Joanna Merwood-Salisbury, *Chicago 1890: The Skyscraper and the Modern City* (Chicago: University of Chicago Press, 2009), pp. 13-54.

[17] "Forward," *Work of Young Architects in the Middle West* (New York: Museum of Modern Art, 1933) [unpaginated manuscript in the Museum of Modern Art Archives]. This MoMA exhibition later became part of the 1933 *Century of Progress Exhibition* in Chicago.

[18] In 1940 Hitchcock curated a MoMA show called *Frank Lloyd Wright, American Architect*, publishing the catalogue as *In the Nature of Materials: The Buildings of Frank Lloyd Wright, 1887-1941* (New York: Duell, Sloan and Pearce, 1942). Terence Riley has described the Museum of Modern Art's role in resuscitating Wright's reputation in, "'Frank Lloyd Wright: Architect,' Visions and Revisions Since 1910," *Museum of Modern Art*, no. 16 (Winter 1993/Spring 1994), pp. 1-5. See also Peter Reed and William Kaizen, eds., "The Show to End all Shows: Frank Lloyd Wright and The Museum of Modern Art, 1940," *Studies in Modern Art*, 8 (Museum of Modern Art: New York, 2004).

[19] These supplements were published as a book: Holger Cahill and Alfred H. Barr Jr., eds., *Art in America in Modern Times* (New York: Reynal and Hitchcock, 1934).

[20] John McAndrew, Scenario for *Evolution of the Skyscraper*, Department of Circulating Exhibitions Records. II.1.56.3 Exhibition 76b. *The Evolution of the Skyscraper*. Museum of Modern Art Archives.

[21] *Three Centuries of American Architecture* [MoMA Exh. #83, February 15-March 15, 1939], Museum of Modern Art Archives. On the museum's wartime collaborations with the various propaganda wings of the United States government, see Staniszewski, *The Power of Display*, pp. 206-259.

[22] Robert M. Fogelson, "The Spectre of Decentralization: Downtown During the Great Depression and World War II," in *Downtown: Its Rise and Fall, 1880-1950* (Yale University Press, 2000), pp. 218-248.

[23] *Brooklyn Daily Eagle* (January 8, 1933).

[24] Leverett S. Lyon, "Economic Problems of American Cities," *American Economic Review*, vol. 32, no. 1. Part 2 (1942), p. 308.

[25] Keith D. Revell, "Law Makes Order: The Search for the Skyscraper Ensemble, 1890–1930," in Roberta Moudry, ed., *The American Skyscraper: Cultural Histories* (Cambridge, UK, and New York: Cambridge University Press, 2005).

[26] Daniel Bluestone describes the way in which the mythology of the Chicago School was instrumental for post-war urban renewal efforts in Chicago itself in "Preservation and Renewal in Post-World War II Chicago." On Johnson's promotion of modern skyscraper design in the post-war era, see the essays by Reinhold Martin and Kazys Varnelis in *Philip Johnson. The Constancy of Change*, pp. 110–119, 120–135.

CHICAGO STYLE

ELLEN D. GRIMES

If architecture once had a Chicago School, we now have a Chicago style. The Hyde Park Art Center, or HPAC – both the building and the organization – is a product of at least four versions of Chicagoism and the instigator of something properly considered a Chicago style. Here's the genealogy (bear with me): Imagists and Alinskyites meet Tigermanism and Deleuzianism. Chicago-style hot dogs, popcorn, softball, stepping, rap, relish, politics, pizza … meet your architecture.

Founded in the 1930s, HPAC was an alternative art venue before the term was invented. Its first building was a bar and the operation was run by a group known as the Monster Roster. They evolved into the Chicago Imagists, and held their "seminal" exhibition, *Hairy Who?* in 1966. They opposed the boring New Yorky-Greenbergian abstractionists. Their work was grotesque, surreal, figural, and hairy.

Since then, HPAC has survived by giving young artists teaching jobs in community programs on the city's South Side while running an adventuresome roster of exhibitions. It's a hustle – producing art and creating an audience for it at the same time. When it came time to leave the smelly, ruinous ballroom of the Del Prado Hotel, HPAC's location since the 1980s, Garofalo was the only choice. He brought Tigermanism and Deleuzianism to the HPAC's Imagists and Alinskyites, and that new matchup produced a loading dock façade, a big blinking screen, a catwalk gallery, classrooms, studios, a sidewalk party space with its own hot dog truck in permanent residence, Sun Ra exhibits with the Jesse White Tumblers in attendance, to name some of it all. HPAC owns only one piece of art, and it is its building.

All of it is Chicago style: the happy and promiscuous commercial appropriation, a relaxed insistence on the beauty of the vulgar, delight in the gizmo's social operation, hyperpragmatic, grotesque, surreal, figural, cool.

ABSORBING ATTENTION

SYLVIA LAVIN

132

City gates have always been points of negotiation between various competing interests: those of the state, the urban inhabitant, the exurban visitor, tourist, soldier, etc. The currency of exchange has also varied, ranging from boiling oil, to taxation, passports, and ticket stubs. One characteristic of this history has been that these currencies have become less and less lethal, and the gates, as a corollary, have become increasingly symbolic and self-contained. Cloud Gate, the thirty-three by sixty-six feet stainless steel sculpture at Millennium Park, intervenes in this trajectory.

It not only suggests that today's systems of security and control are so pervasive and amorphous that they can only be recognized if given the identity of their hypothetical antithesis, the undisciplined cloud, but it also absorbs into its perfectly seamless and uninterrupted siren call the one thing the contemporary subject might still be said to possess: her attention.

CLOUD GATE, ANISH KAPOOR, 2006.

ADMIRATION AND APPREHENSION OF THE AMERICAN METROPOLIS

EUROPEAN RESPONSES TO THE *PLAN OF CHICAGO*

DAVID H. HANEY

The *Plan of Chicago* was published in 1909 as a luxuriously illustrated volume intended not merely as a factual presentation of practical planning concepts, but also, and more importantly, as propaganda to arouse public support for civic improvement.[1] The prominent Chicago architect Daniel H. Burnham and his colleagues in the elite Commercial Club were the authors of the *Plan*, which they saw as an overall solution to problems of traffic congestion, unhealthy environmental conditions, and haphazard development. Burnham's first major planning project had been the World's Columbian Exposition of 1893, where he oversaw the vast array of logistical and design solutions necessary to create the dazzling spectacle dubbed the "White City."[2] The architecture of the Columbian Exposition was symbolized by the neo-classical "Court of Honor" with its gleaming white, electrically-lit façades, which stood in strong contrast to the chaos and grime of the surrounding city. Burnham's planning style was characterized by neo-classical architecture arranged around grand axes and monumental spaces, recalling the planning principles of the French Baroque. This success led to a number of other urban planning commissions for Burnham, most notably the restoration and renewal of the eighteenth-century plan by Pierre Charles L'Enfant for Washington DC.[3]

Unsurprisingly, news of the *Plan* soon reached professional circles in Western Europe through publications and exhibitions; Burnham even traveled across the Atlantic to promote its ideas personally. To many Europeans, America, and Chicago in particular, represented the best and the worst of modern industrial metropolitan society. During this period reformers on both sides of the Atlantic were appalled by living conditions caused by a dangerous increase in traffic levels, overbuilding, and lack of fresh air and sunshine. Many critics blamed these adverse developments on uncontrolled commercialism, capitalism, and industrialization. The birth of metropolitan mass-culture was both welcomed and feared. On the one hand, the potentially grand scale of construction and planning made possible by industrial organization was celebrated; on the other, the danger of depersonalization brought about by mass-production and mass-consumption caused deep concern.

Burnham was famous for his statement that only "big" plans would stir the imagination and the *Plan* was a strategy for harnessing the potential of the colossal metropolis in an organized and aesthetically pleasing manner. The artist Jules Guerin's striking color perspectives emphasized the vast scale of the *Plan* through depictions of grand axial streets stretching out into the distant prairie, a vision which could not fail to instill a sense of awe. At the same time, these images of Chicago as a symbol of American mass-culture and commercial success also aroused a sense of apprehension among some Europeans. The members of the Commercial Club were indeed the heads of great commercial interests, and although their intentions may have been noble, they nevertheless were ultimately serving the same American capitalist interests that had resulted in chaotic urban conditions in the first place.

The *Plan* also raised questions about the relation of the modern metropolis to history and national culture. Burnham clearly wanted to bring what he understood to be the civilizing influence of European high culture to Chicago through the adaptation of Baroque and neo-classical planning and architecture to modern American needs. In the narrative description of the published *Plan of Chicago*, Paris was held up as the ideal city for emulation. The level of imitation was especially obvious in Guerin's illustration of a new Chicago opera house, nearly a direct copy of the one in Paris. However, Burnham's plan expanded the extent and size of avenues and civic spaces far beyond what would have been possible within European cities such as Paris, London, or Berlin. The popular press in Chicago was convinced that not only was their city capable of successfully emulating European models, but moreover that the *Plan* had actually transcended them. From the [Chicago] *Daily News* in 1910 we read: "Jealous Paris Fears Chicago Beauty Plan: D. H. Burnham says French capital dreads American city will snatch its laurels."[4] And the following year the *Chicago Record-Herald* proclaimed: "Model of Kaiser for New Berlin is 'Chicago Plan:' German Emperor has Commission Adopt Burnham Ideas for His Capital."[5] The bombast of such headlines points to the pride with which many Chicagoans viewed the *Plan* and, indeed, it provoked a remarkable degree of attention from professionals in Europe.

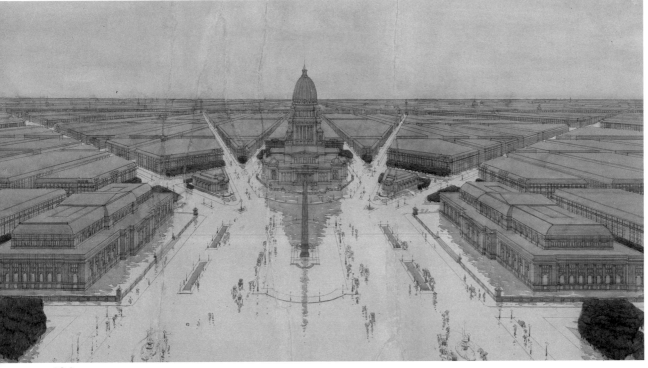

136 PROPOSED CIVIC CENTER FROM THE *PLAN OF CHICAGO* BY DANIEL H. BURNHAM AND EDWARD H. BENNETT, REPRODUCED FOR GERMAN READERS BY WERNER HEGEMANN IN *DER NEUE BEBAUUNGSPLAN FÜR CHICAGO*, 1910. HEGEMANN EMPHASIZED THAT THE *PLAN* WOULD CREATE MONUMENTAL PUBLIC SPACES, PARTICULARLY AT STREET INTERSECTIONS.

RECEPTION OF THE *PLAN OF CHICAGO* IN LONDON, BERLIN, AND PARIS

One of the most important events in the newly emerging field of city planning was the 1910 International Town Planning Conference held by the Royal Institute of British Architects in London. The *Plan of Chicago* was prominently exhibited there through models, drawings, and the enormous painted views by Jules Guerin. The proceedings of the conference, including audience reactions to Burnham's own talk, were published in a thick volume.[6] Judging from these proceedings, some Englishmen greeted Burnham and the *Plan* with great enthusiasm as harbingers of modernization, while others viewed them with great suspicion as representatives of American commercial interests. English architects and planners had already divided into these two camps well before the publication of the *Plan*, and their conflicting views pointed to fundamental differences between those advocating large-scale planning in service of the collective needs of the metropolis, and those who believed that small-scale neighborhood planning was necessary to protect against the alienation of mass-culture. These two positions could be conveniently represented by those in favor of wide streets and monumental buildings, versus those promoting small-scale picturesque planning and the English garden city movement.[7] The former railed against the insularity of their countrymen, and the latter held themselves to be the protectors of English individualism.

137 PROPOSED OPERA HOUSE FROM THE *PLAN OF CHICAGO* BY DANIEL H. BURNHAM AND EDWARD H. BENNETT, REPRODUCED FOR GERMAN READERS BY WERNER HEGEMANN IN *DER NEUE BEBAUUNGSPLAN FÜR CHICAGO*, 1910.

Naturally, Burnham's own talk at the London conference generated much discussion.[8] Rather than elaborating upon the *Plan of Chicago* itself, or even on specific design strategies, Burnham turned to the broader theme of "democracy" and the type of organization needed to bring large-scale schemes to realization. Burnham went to great lengths to defend American democracy as a system whereby a few civic-minded individuals could serve the needs of the mass public. He explained that, "the town-planning men in every city are the ablest in the community," in reference to the leaders of the largest businesses and enterprises.[9] Another important factor in American democracy was "publicity," which for Burnham meant that, "with us any degree of secrecy in governmental politics is impossible."[10] American political leaders could thus not foist a grand scheme upon the public against its will, as despots had been able to do in the past. Burnham concluded his talk by discussing the need for better use of resources and lauding the advent of electric power, for it would mean the demise of the pollution caused by horse traffic and coal smoke.

In the discussion that immediately followed, audience comments on Burnham's talk were generally positive with some exceptions. The planner and university professor Stanley Adshead was unequivocally supportive, recognizing that America and Chicago offered a genuinely new culture and need not imitate European cultural models. Indeed, Adshead saw only a progressive modernizing tendency in Burnham's work:

A great city must be built on a great scale; it must have wide streets, wide sidewalks, and big buildings simply composed; it must concentrate its interest at points, and must not spread it about with reckless waste. I do not look disparagingly ahead; on every side I see evidence of the need for improvement, and the advent of the Ritz Hotel and Selfridge's Store marks a change.[11]

Selfridge's department store in central London was indeed a "big building" designed by Burnham himself for the American retailer Gordon Selfridge, and the store was a symbol of the kind of American commercialism for which Chicago was known. Adshead's comment about "reckless waste" was directed against garden city advocates like the socialist architect Raymond Unwin who were arguing for decentralization.

Predictably, the founder of the English garden city movement, Ebenezer Howard, made no reference at all to Chicago following Burnham's talk. Others were openly critical; one participant noted that:

[...] the tendency of to-day was, in towns [...] to substitute the benevolent despotism of the great landlords [with] an organized democracy. That would appear to be what Mr. Burnham wants, and, to my thinking, it is one of the very worst things that could possibly happen to the people.[12]

Another speaker observed that a few elite men could in fact make decisions without consulting the majority, which he also believed to be happening in America. Between them, these two English critics identified what they perceived to be the twin flaws of American culture: on the one hand, a democracy of the masses who could not be trusted because they were ill-informed, and on the other, business elites who could not be trusted because they were acting in their own favor in the name of the masses.

In the English professional press at the time, other criticisms were more practical: "Grandiose as it appears on paper [...] considerable doubt may be pardoned to an Englishman as to how it would work in practice."[13] The review of the exhibition published in the official proceedings also expressed a lack of conviction: "In considering the proposals as a whole, however, we cannot help feeling a doubt as to whether the effects indicated in the drawings are ever likely to be attained in actuality."[14] English skepticism was no doubt based on over two centuries of unrealized urban proposals for London, beginning with Christopher Wren's plan for the city following the Great Fire of 1666. Although the immediate impact of the *Plan* was limited in Britain, the discussion surrounding it revealed underlying conflicts between big money and planning on the one hand, and smaller-scale, more socially responsible approaches on the other, that would be central to the subsequent development of city planning.

Another series of grand schemes on display at the 1910 exhibition in London presented the "Competition for a Plan for the Development of Greater Berlin," which had been judged in March of that year before the London exhibition had opened in October.[15] The catalyst for the 1910 RIBA conference was in fact a 1909 German Garden City Association study tour to England, widely hailed as a success in both countries.[16]

While the garden city idea had taken firm root in Germany, planners and architects there were divided along lines similar to those in England. Significantly, the competition for Greater Berlin was conceived by advocates of monumental planning; one of the three organizers, Albert Hofmann, even made reference to the "White City" of the Columbian Exposition as a commendable precedent.[17] Hofmann recognized that Berlin was a different city from other European capitals as it had experienced the most rapid growth of any on the Continent in the late nineteenth century. While there were significant eighteenth-century urban spaces in Berlin such as the grand avenue Unter den Linden, on the whole it had become a nineteenth-century city dominated by speculative development. The plan for Berlin was intended to restore a sense of European monumentality, while also solving technical problems such as traffic flow. Designers entering the Berlin planning competition faced similar problems to those of Burnham and his team.

Among the Berlin competition winners, fourth place was awarded to the team of architect Bruno Schmitz, planner Otto Blum, and engineers Havestadt & Contag.[18] This scheme received great praise in the professional press, and among the prize winners it was thought by many to most closely resemble the *Plan of Chicago*. One of the focal points of the scheme was a proposed "Forum of Labor" located on an island in the Spree River, reminiscent of the governmental "Civic Center" depicted in the *Plan of Chicago*.[19] This scheme also incorporated broad avenues and monumental public spaces, designed to represent the relatively new imperial status of Berlin as a capital. Furthermore, the scheme by Schmitz used a series of free-standing high-rise blocks, which one critic, Albert Brinckmann, decried as "American," associated as they were

139 with Chicago commercialism.[20] To such critics, this kind of gesture was not suitable for imperial Berlin. Nevertheless, Brinckmann found the Schmitz scheme sufficiently monumental to elevate it from the fate of being too American, "even though [the] design is reminiscent of projects such as the development plan for Chicago."[21] As was the case in England, Chicago was here too a symbolic entity evoking different and sometimes contradictory responses.

Perhaps the most important single European professional in this era to promote the *Plan*, and American planning ideas in general, was the economist and planner Werner Hegemann.[22] He had spent a number of years in the US, principally in Boston, Chicago, and Philadelphia, and thus was an authority on the subject of American planning. He was the primary organizer of the Berlin City Planning Exhibition in the spring of 1910, as well as of a similar follow-up exhibition that was opened in Düsseldorf that summer. For the latter exhibition, Hegemann succeeded in persuading Burnham to ship the large-scale Guerin paintings for the *Plan* across the Atlantic. (Because of this, they could be displayed later in London.) Hegemann correctly believed that the stunning Guerin paintings would be a sensation at the exhibition, winning the public over to the cause of urban planning. Afterwards, he published an extensive two-volume catalogue of the 1910 exhibitions that he had organized, as well as a small booklet dedicated specifically to the *Plan*.[23]

In his brochure on Chicago, Hegemann did not discuss the organizational and political structures behind the realization of the *Plan*, but focused on its formal and aesthetic qualities. He announced in the opening: "All of Chicago – not just a limited exhibition area – is to be treated as a magnificent overall design, and be created anew as the most beautiful city on the continent, perhaps in the world."[24] For Hegemann the significance of the *Plan* was its comprehensiveness, not just as a matter of practical problem solving, but also on the artistic level; although he did not state it as such, he clearly thought of it as a kind of *Gesamtkunstwerk*. For him, the *Plan* represented "an attempt for once, to see the entire city organism first and foremost from the standpoint of the architecturally oriented city planner."[25] Here he implied that the "architecturally oriented" planner would have an aesthetically more sensitive perspective than the technically oriented engineer, who was often in charge of laying out streets at this time. He was particularly impressed by the open spaces in the *Plan*, not simply the wide, open streets. He noted that the "monumental representation of the city would primarily occur at the street intersections," with the Civic Center at the most important intersection providing the focal point of the whole.[26] He did not fear the sense of monotony that some of his English colleagues did, for he believed that the *Plan* was also well-considered at the level of detail. Unlike many of his German colleagues, Hegemann felt that the *Plan* presented a legitimate model for his countrymen to follow.

THE CHICAGO PARK SYSTEM AS SEEN BY EUROPEAN PLANNERS AND LANDSCAPE ARCHITECTS

During this period the emerging fields of urban planning and landscape architecture often overlapped. While Europeans had made great progress in the field of park design and green space planning, many continued to recognize the park systems of American cities as being at the forefront of the field. The two US cities that received the most praise for their parks were Boston and Chicago. The Metropolitan Park System of Boston, consisting of large landscape reserves surrounding the city, was seen as an example of urban green space planning on a metropolitan or regional scale. By contrast, even though the parks of Chicago were part of a large overall system, they were generally praised for their individual character and contribution to neighborhood life.

In 1905, four years before the publication of the *Plan*, the Parisian landscape architect J. C. N. Forestier penned a small brochure, *Grandes villes et systèmes de parcs* (Large Cities and Park Systems), with the problem of the planning of Paris in the background.[27] Forestier included a statistical table comparing the ratio of park area to population among sixteen major international cities.[28] Not insignificantly, all the examples that he gave were American except for three: Vienna, London, and Paris, with Paris having the lowest ratio on the list. Paris was in a different situation from most other European capitals, as Forestier noted, because the ring of fortifications surrounding it still had not been demolished, which caused considerable planning problems. Despite his obvious admiration for American urban park systems, there appears to have been some irritation underlying his comment that "some Americans" thought that Paris was a "finished city."[29] While it is not clear whether Forestier was referring directly to Burnham and his colleagues, his observation was certainly applicable. In the *Plan of Chicago*, the model city of Paris is primarily the nineteenth-century city of

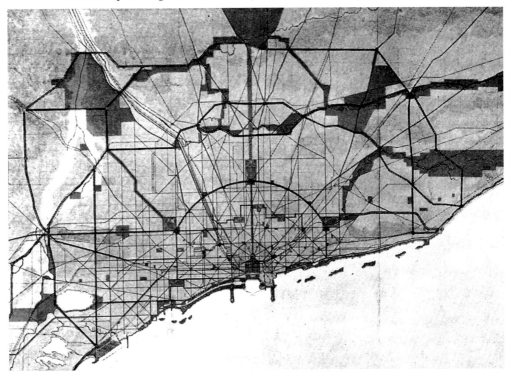

141   MAP OF CHICAGO'S PARK SYSTEM FROM THE *PLAN OF CHICAGO* BY DANIEL H. BURNHAM AND EDWARD H. BENNETT, REPRODUCED FOR GERMAN READERS BY WERNER HEGEMANN IN *DER NEUE BEBAUUNGSPLAN FÜR CHICAGO.*

Haussmann and his boulevards, not the congested early-twentieth-century Paris of Forestier's time. Following this comment, Forestier elaborated: "The city that ceases is the city that is beginning to die; in order to live, it must develop. Now Paris is still living, and with more vigor than ever."[30]

Forestier further noted that the growth of Paris was primarily taking place in the suburbs beyond the old fortification walls. Therefore, green space planning for Paris needed to consider the entire metropolitan region, not just the urban core. Ironically perhaps, while Burnham was extolling the charms of historic Paris as the model for modern Chicago, Forestier was trying to explain that Paris itself was suffering from uncontrolled metropolitan growth. Forestier, however, did not make any derisive comments about Chicago, instead he praised its inner city parks as being of great benefit to the population on a daily basis.

In 1911, Hegemann published a study with the title *Ein Parkbuch: Amerikanische Parkanlagen* (A Park Book: American Park Facilities).[31] Once again, the cities of Boston and Chicago were the primary examples, but this time he focused solely on green spaces, including the existing parks within the three Chicago Commission districts, as well as the new lakefront parks proposed by Burnham and his colleagues. Hegemann was particularly interested in a type of small park for

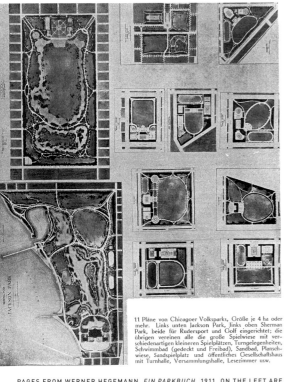

11 Pläne von Chicagoer Volksparks, Größe je 4 ha oder mehr. Links unten Jackson Park, links oben Sherman Park, beide für Rudersport und Golf eingerichtet; die übrigen vereinen alle die große Spielwiese mit verschiedenartigen kleineren Spielplätzen, Turngelegenheiten, Schwimmbad (gedeckt und Freibad), Sandbad, Planschwiese, Sandspielplatz und öffentliches Gesellschaftshaus mit Turnhalle, Versammlungshalle, Lesezimmer usw.

Schafherde im Washington Park, Anschauungsunterricht für Großstadtkinder.

Planschwiese im Mark White Park. Im Hintergrund rechts ein öffentliches Gesellschaftshaus.

Kinderreigen beim Frühlingsfest.

Schotten in Nationaltracht beim Frühlingsfest.

PAGES FROM WERNER HEGEMANN, *EIN PARKBUCH*, 1911. ON THE LEFT ARE PLANS OF THE SMALL PARKS THAT THE OLMSTED BROTHERS DESIGNED FOR CHICAGO, WHICH HEGEMANN SAW AS EXAMPLES OF RATIONAL, SOCIALLY RESPONSIBLE DESIGN. THE PHOTOGRAPHS AT CENTER AND RIGHT ILLUSTRATE VARIOUS ACTIVITIES IN CHICAGO PARKS THAT HEGEMANN CELEBRATED.

active recreation specifically developed for Chicago by the Olmsted firm in Boston.[32] Hegemann referred to these as *"Spielparks"* (play parks). These Chicago neighborhood parks were smaller than the older landscape parks, and Hegemann emphasized that every space within them was designed for a specific recreational function.[33] More unique to Chicago were the "field houses" specifically conceived for this park type in order to provide indoor recreational space during the long Chicago winters. In his study, Hegemann featured exterior photos of these buildings along with outdoor gymnasiums and swimming pools. For Hegemann, these parks provided supportive environments for the phenomenon of cultural diversity in America, as symbolized by the organized public festivals staged on their grounds:

Chicago is one of the largest immigrant population centers in the world, and here all conceivable peoples are brought together in a spirit of communal happiness; one cannot imagine anything more reassuring than these great fraternal festivals, where each people strives to show off its most beautiful assets.[34]

To illustrate his remarks, he included photos of activities such as children engaged in a great circle dance and young women performing in kilts and silk stockings, the latter captioned "Scotts in their native costume."[35]

Hegemann's *Parkbuch* concluded with a small section featuring the garden and park designs of the Hamburg firm of Jacob Ochs, who had financed the publication. All of the illustrated designs and writing in this section bear the mark of Leberecht Migge, the leading landscape architect in the Ochs firm. Migge was a close colleague of

Sandspielplatz vor einem öffentlichen Gesellschaftshause in einem Volkspark Chicagos.

Mädchen im Schwimmbad in einem Volkspark Chicagos.

143

Hegemann and was deeply influenced by his thinking. In 1913, Migge published his own book on landscape theory and design titled *Gartenkultur des 20. Jahrhunderts* (Garden Culture of the 20th Century).[36] American parks played an important role in Migge's book, again primarily those in Boston and Chicago.[37] His study was more analytical than Hegemann's, as he tried to explain more specifically how American models might be adapted to German culture. Highly enthusiastic about the rational layouts of the small Chicago parks designed by the Olmsted brothers, Migge interpreted the repetitive forms and spatial organizations of these parks in the context of the German Werkbund discussion of "types" as essential spatial units. He believed that through a system of spatial types, park designs could be rationally assembled almost like a kit of parts. Migge was probably thinking of these small Chicago parks when he wrote that it would be up to Germans, "to contribute music institutes, public schools, and open air museums, as supplements to the sport halls and public libraries of the Americans, as possible intellectual additions to these green gymnasiums."[38] He further commented on the need for Germans to improve the American park models in an architectural sense: "[...] if we term the sober and unimaginative park architecture of the Americans simply rational, then may our later social park period be called upon to promise the highest values: it should be monumental."[39] While Migge admired the practicality of Chicago and its park designs, he also believed that Germany, as a European country, possessed a higher level of culture.

THE CAPITALIST METROPOLIS

Given that European discussions of the *Plan of Chicago* and the city's parks were largely based on published material, it is unsurprising that many criticisms were superficial. The European sense of cultural superiority asserted by Migge and others was to some degree disingenuous. Berlin, for example, despite being the imperial capital, was largely an industrial city with masses of workers crowded into substandard housing.

The German Kaiser and leading German architects would have naturally wanted to conceal this fact by creating new monumental spaces and buildings. Thus their assertion of the need for monumentality during this period was also a reflection of cultural insecurity within their own society. In France, meanwhile, Forestier complained that Americans thought of the city of Paris as a finished work of art, when in fact it was a vast, rapidly growing metropolis extending well beyond the old fortifications. Burnham's own optimism and his somewhat condescending remarks to his London colleagues were based on another cliché, that because the American city was relatively new it could be more easily redesigned than its European counterparts. To some degree this was true, but the implementation of the *Plan of Chicago* proved to be quite difficult. Michigan Avenue, for example, was widened and extended only after protracted legal battles with individual landowners and proposals for the construction of a great Civic Center, and the transformation of Congress Street into a monumental east-west thoroughfare were never carried out.[40] However, although the search for individual European identities in architectural discourse has long ceased to be an issue, and "Americanism" is no longer synonymous with mass-commercialism, capitalist metropolises around the world continue to inspire both awe and derision. The *Plan of Chicago* stands out as one of the first attempts to give the capitalist metropolis a global identity and thus remains a milestone in international histories of economic forces and urban form.

NOTES

[1] Daniel H. Burnham and Edward H. Bennett, *Plan of Chicago* (Chicago: The Commercial Club, 1909). See also the online version accessed via the *Encyclopedia of Chicago*, at http://www.enclyclopedia.chicagohistory. org/pages/10417.html. For the standard comprehensive study, see Carl Smith, *The Plan of Chicago: Daniel Burnham and the Remaking of the American City* (Chicago: The University of Chicago Press, 2006).

[2] Smith, *The Plan of Chicago*, pp. 19-22.

[3] Ibid., pp. 22-23.

[4] Papers of Daniel H. Burnham, Ryerson and Burnham Archives of the Art Institute of Chicago, Call number: 1943.1, Box 62, Folder 36, Series VIII, *Chicago Daily News*, October 26, 1910.

[5] Papers of Daniel H. Burnham, Ryerson and Burnham Archives of the Art Institute of Chicago, Call number: 1943, 1, Box FF62.36, *The Chicago Record-Herald*, January 14, 1911.

[6] William Whyte, ed., *The Transactions of the Royal Institute of British Architects Town Planning Conference, London 10-15 October 1910* [Reprint] (London, New York: Routledge, 2011).

[7] Ibid., *Transactions*, introduction.

[8] Lecture by Daniel H. Burnham, "A City of the Future Under a Democratic Government" in Whyte, *Transactions*, pp. 368-378.

[9] Ibid., p. 370.

[10] Ibid., pp. 368-369.

[11] Ibid., p. 502.

[12] Ibid., p. 394.

[13] Ibid., [p. vii]; NB: there are no page numbers in Whyte's introduction.

[14] Ibid., p. 738.

[15] Ibid., [p. vii].

[16] Whyte, *Transactions*, [p. iv]; No author, *Aus Englischen Gartenstädten* (Berlin: Deutsche Gartenstadt-Gesellschaft, Renaissance-Verlag, 1910).

[17] Wolfgang Sonne, *Representing the State: Capital City Planning in the Early Twentieth Century* (Munich: Prestel, 2003), p. 104.

[18] Ibid., p. 117.

[19] Ibid., p. 119.

[20] Ibid., p. 120.

[21] Ibid., p. 120.

[22] Christiane Crasemann Collins, *Werner Hegemann and the Search for Universal Urbanism* (New York: W. W. Norton, 2005).

[23] Werner Hegemann, *Der Städtebau* (Berlin: Wasmuth, vol. 1, 1911, vol. 2, 1913); Werner Hegemann, *Der neue Bebauungsplan für Chicago* (Berlin: Wasmuth, 1910).

[24] Ibid., p. 5.

[25] Ibid., p. 25.

[26] Ibid., p. 14.

[27] J. C. N. Forestier, *Grandes Villes et Systèmes de Parcs* (Paris: Hachette, 1906).

[28] Ibid., p. 44.

[29] Ibid., p. 49.

[30] Ibid., p. 49.

[31] Werner Hegemann, *Ein Parkbuch: Amerikanische Parkanlagen* (Berlin: Wasmuth, 1911).

[32] William Tippens, "The Olmsted Brothers in the Midwest: Naturalism, Formalism, and The City Beautiful Movement," in William H. Tishler, ed., *Midwestern Landscape Architecture* (Urbana: University of Illinois Press, 2000), pp. 159–173.

[33] Ibid., p. 9.

[34] Ibid., p. 10.

[35] Ibid., plates between pp. 8–9.

[36] David H. Haney, trans., ed., Leberecht Migge, *Garden Culture of the Twentieth Century* (Washington, DC: Dumbarton Oaks, 2013). Original edition: Leberecht Migge, *Gartenkultur des 20. Jahrhunderts* (Jena: Diederichs, 1913). See also David H. Haney, *When Modern Was Green: Life and Work of Landscape Architect Leberecht Migge* (Abingdon, UK: Routledge, 2010); another important study of Chicago parks by a German landscape architect during the period is Hugo Koch, *Gartenkunst im Städtebau* (Berlin: Wasmuth, 1914).

[37] For example, plate 4 in the appendix in Migge's *Gartenkultur* is of an unidentified plan of one of the small Olmsted parks, in fact Davis Square in the Back of Yards district in Chicago.

[38] Leberecht Migge, *Garden Culture of the Twentieth Century*, p. 27.

[39] Ibid., p. 28.

[40] Smith, *The Plan of Chicago*, pp. 134–135, 138.

A TALE OF TWO PAVILIONS

MARK LEE

When it comes to the archetype of the primitive hut, nothing is more elemental than the model of two identical horizontal planes separated vertically to define a space between. From Laugier to Loos to Le Corbusier, one can discern a historical line of development as to how the planes are supported and the space between is defined.

UNStudio's 2009 Burnham Centennial Pavilion fits squarely into this lineage. Designed as a folly in Millennium Park, the pavilion consists of two planes connected by three curvilinear legs around its center. The first plane, which is slightly lifted off the ground, defines the podium; the second plane, which is clearly levitated, defines the roof. Within this contained volume, space extends horizontally at the perimeter and vertically through the three roof openings defined by the legs that obliquely frame the Chicago skyline.

Not far from the Burnham Pavilion – about sixty miles west and designed about sixty years earlier – stands Mies van der Rohe's Farnsworth House, the quintessential model for the modern primitive hut consisting of two horizontal planes as well. While both are buildings of the same genre, they represent opposite spatial predilections. Farnsworth is levitated within a natural landscape while the Burnham pavilion is anchored within the city grid. Farnsworth's shifted core projects a centrifugal spatial extension, while the pavilion's centripetal core grounds its center. Farnsworth is non-directional and could be turned upside down; the pavilion is upside down with the "floor" supported by three legs that barely touch the podium, allowing the base to become a ceiling of lights.

At a time when everything seems to be moving in the direction of fluidity, the attributes presented by the Burnham Pavilion – grounded, centripetal, and upside down – announce the possibility of a primitive hut of the not-too-distant future.

NEITHER DUCK NOR SHED
ANDRES LEPIK

The skyscraper as a new architectural typology started its development in Chicago and, with its Sears Tower (now: Willis Tower), the city kept the title for the world's tallest skyscraper for twenty-five years. After all the countless copies of Mies van der Rohe's Seagram Tower in the 1960s and 1970s that spread worldwide and the banalities of post-modernist high-rises in the 1980s and 1990s, it seemed already as if the design of skyscrapers was reduced to a handful of basic ideas that had been developed a long time ago. The only remaining challenge was to solve the engineering problems necessary to win the next height record. The Aqua Tower points in a different direction. While its core remains to follow the economic forces that shape all contemporary skyscrapers globally, it introduces one radical innovation: the swelling floor slabs that extend to balconies on its façade. While the open spaces on the exterior seem to take their inspiration from the balconies of Bertrand Goldberg's wonderful Marina Towers of 1962 (which are close by), the Aqua Tower with its irregular curves creates an highly dynamic effect. Following the terminology of Venturi and Scott Brown, the Aqua Tower is neither a "decorated shed" (such as Philip Johnson's AT&T Building in New York) nor is it a "duck" like the CCTV Tower by Rem Koolhaas (for whom Jeanne Gang, principal of Studio Gang, worked for some time). It shows that skyscraper design can still offer more than records in height.

AQUA TOWER. STUDIO GANG ARCHITECTS. 2010.

NO FAILURE TOO GREAT

ALEXANDER EISENSCHMIDT

1871 was the year in which the cities of Berlin and Chicago were catapulted into a modern reality. That year the Chicago Fire inspired a building code that in combination with advances in fireproofing iron and steel-frames and inventions such as Otis's safety passenger elevator guided the construction of a new city with massive buildings that soon lined entire blocks of the downtown grid. On the other side of the Atlantic, Berlin's emergence as the capital of the Second German Empire shifted the political, economic, and cultural landscape of Germany and Europe and established the city as a metropolis. But, whereas most Chicagoans wholeheartedly embraced their involuntary new urban beginning and even declared that the city "could not afford to do without the Chicago Fire," Berliners observed "the sudden change within the city from provincialism to its international standing" with less confidence in the opportunities presented by the new metropolitan condition.[1]

As Berliners learned more about Chicago's rapid urban development, however, they became increasingly fascinated by the metropolis in the Midwestern plains and began to see a relationship between the two cities, understanding their own metropolitan fate in the trajectory of Chicago. While Chicago was unique, its development was understood as an indicator of the future. The ur-metropolis, with its unconditional commitment to progress, dedication to technology, willingness to stage experiments, and ability to continuously reinvent itself, eventually stood as a model for Berlin that, once it caught up with American modernity, was to find its own metropolitan traits. The interaction between the two cities not only offered a productive urban analogy that pointed to what the future might hold, but the conflation of one urbanism into another (projecting Chicago onto Berlin) also prompted an early iteration of "metropolitan architecture" and, eventually, pointed towards a new kind of architecture-city relationship that rethought the metropolis as a catalytic realm of invention and a space of possibilities. Chicago was able to accelerate out of conditions that Berlin saw as disastrous, making it the perfect model to re-evaluate Berlin's apparent failures as opportunities.

A NEW KIND OF CITY

Developing gradually from a small town that was first mentioned in 1244, Berlin's nineteenth-century growth took place at an unprecedented pace, accelerated by the city's new function as a capital and culminating in what early travel guides would declare to be the "greatest purely modern city in Europe."[2] From 1871 to 1895, the population of Berlin doubled from 820,000 to 1.6 million, an influx that new construction efforts could not match, resulting in a population density that reached its all-time high in 1900 when an average of 29,750 individuals lived on

151

one square kilometer. While the city experienced enormous urban pressures, it had become the "centre of technological, civilizing modernity" in Europe, whose people followed the development "with a mixture of horror and fascination."[3] Returning to Berlin even after a short trip abroad, many expressed that "so much has changed [...] it is as if one were in a strange city."[4]

In this climate, cultural critics sought to understand the dilemmas and potentials of modernity and its effects on Berlin, and protagonists of the newly emerging discipline of *Städtebau* (urban planning) sought to find scientific rules for the study and reorganization of a rapidly expanding city. Planner and engineer Reinhard Baumeister, for example, sponsored a unified building law for the German Empire in 1871 and published the influential book *Stadterweiterungen in technischer, baupolizeilicher und wirtschaftlicher Beziehung* (City-Expansions in Relation to Technology, Building Safety Laws, and Economy) in 1876.[5] What traumatized planners and common Berliners alike was that the city had not only changed dramatically, but had also become unrecognizable through the implementation of new urban forms, new means of mobility, and a new demographic diversity with an increasing number of foreigners. While this was common for metropolises in the United States, it appeared threatening to the German capital; to cite one reference from a widely read text by the conservative historian Julius Langbehn, "the capital grew in the last century at such a rate only comparable to the cities of North America."[6]

The "lightning city," as Chicago was called for its fast development in popular accounts of the 1870s, was on most minds when making this comparison.[7] The city that in

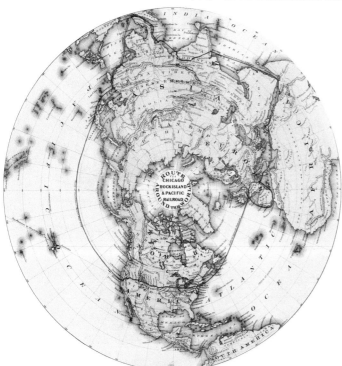

152 MAP OF THE RAILWAY AND STEAMER ROUTES AROUND THE WORLD, PRODUCED BY THE CHICAGO ROCK ISLAND AND PACIFIC RAILROAD, 1870. ZOOMING OUT FROM THE CITY'S LOCAL CONTEXT IN THE MIDDLE OF THE MIDWESTERN PLAINS, THIS MAP CELEBRATES THE CITY'S CENTRAL POSITION AND STATUS AS AN INFRASTRUCTURAL HUB CONNECTED TO THE REST OF THE WORLD – A METROPOLIS SIMULTANEOUSLY IN THE MIDDLE OF NOWHERE AND AT THE CENTER OF THE WORLD.

the early nineteenth century existed only as a frontier village with a few settlers, had materialized by 1870 as one of the largest markets, supported by the world's most active railroad junction and a harbor that connected the center of the US with the rest of the Western world and beyond. By 1890, its population had long passed the one-million mark and it sprawled over more than 180 square miles, making it the city with the largest footprint in the world. For contemporary observers, Chicago had outpaced progress in the sense that it forged ahead without weighing options or theorizing potential outcomes.[8] The city's central business district was regarded as the strongest expression of economic pressures, the dismissal of art and tradition, the embrace of technological developments, and the rapid implementation of new forms (from tools to buildings). Rather than understanding the quick, uncompromising, and concentrated implementations of modern life and form as a result of nineteenth-century pressures, Europeans saw Chicago's development as a forecast of the new century.[9] In Chicago, the future had arrived in the present.

A COMPOUNDED METROPOLIS

Berlin, in particular, was receptive to images of this American city. From officials to urban theorists and cultural critics, Berlin was viewed as an odd European city in its embrace of uncompromising modernity and its seeming acceptance of American

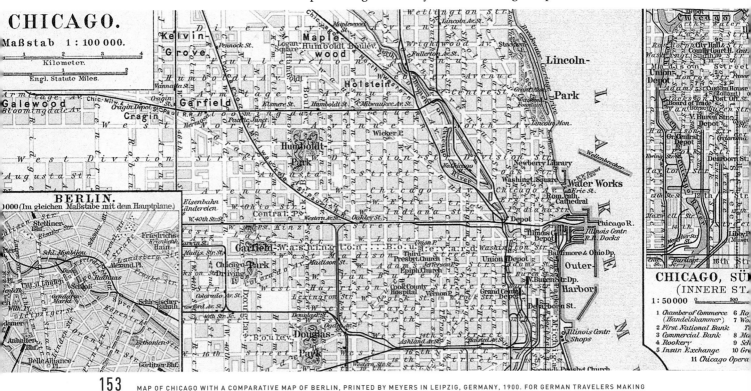

153 MAP OF CHICAGO WITH A COMPARATIVE MAP OF BERLIN, PRINTED BY MEYERS IN LEIPZIG, GERMANY, 1900. FOR GERMAN TRAVELERS MAKING THEIR WAY THROUGH CHICAGO, THIS MAP OFFERED A CONSTANT REMINDER OF THE INTIMATE RELATIONSHIP BETWEEN THE TWO CITIES AND A MEANS OF VISUALIZING A "GERMAN" CHICAGO AND AN "AMERICAN" BERLIN.

influences. As many compared Berlin to the urban growth of cities within the US, they referred not only to statistical similarities but hinted at a cultural practice that the British journalist and political activist William Thomas Stead in 1901 called "Americanization."[10] What Stead described as a homogenizing force that had reached Europe and might eventually encompass the world, was widely discussed at the turn of the

century with an eye towards rationalized modernization and its alienating consequences on society. Chicago was often understood as its source, for it was not only the
most developed form of North American urbanization but was also seen as a model
that could be repeated. While the general use of the term "Americanization" was
dominated by stereotypes that described the American city as superficial, uniform,
trivial, and without tradition and history (all in all, viewed as the ultimate malfunction
of culture), the often-cited connections and comparisons between Berlin and Chicago
would prove particularly productive as they enabled a repositioning of the city's
failings.

One such productive reworking of Berlin's "problems" through Chicago's
modernity was Walther Rathenau's ironically titled essay "Die schönste Stadt der Welt"
(The Most Beautiful City of the World). Arguing that modern "Berlin did not grow
but transform," Rathenau suggested that the city had not organically evolved over time
but rapidly mutated into a construct similar to North American cities, driven by

154 TRAFFIC INTERSECTION ON DEARBORN AND RANDOLPH STREET, CHICAGO, 1909. THE PANDEMONIUM OF TRAFFIC WAS VIEWED BY MOST WITH A MIXTURE OF REPULSION AND ALLURE

modern forces of mechanization and spectacle.[11] The essay paired harsh criticism
of matter-of-fact urbanity, architecture, and culture with a determined affection
towards progress. Rathenau, himself a product of the modern metropolis (an industrial-
ist, politician, and later statesman), summarized Berlin's situation with the now famous
words: "Athens on the River Spree is dead while Chicago on the Spree is rising."[12]
A new Berlin had emerged that no longer conformed to traditional European conventions, and Chicago became the comparative model for grasping the city's development,
which otherwise remained mysterious.

While it was surprising to many that the quintessential American metropolis could become the model for Berlin, the turn of the century would see a heightened interest in this comparison. Insiders and outsiders alike presented Chicago as a city through which to better understand the German metropolis. Even visitors from the US were compelled to relate the two cities. Mark Twain, who knew Berlin from descriptions in books, recognized Chicago when arriving in the capital. For him, "Berlin had disappeared" and re-emerged as the "European Chicago." The two cities now competed in regards to their flatness, swiftness, constant growth, and newness. The latter contest, Twain reports, was already won by Berlin, which was "the newest city [he] has ever seen," making "Chicago seem venerable beside it."[13] His knowledge of Chicago enabled him to judge Berlin as a city where the streets were wider and straighter than anywhere else, buildings were "architectural Gibraltars," and the bureaucratic organization was unmatched.

155   VIEW FROM POTSDAMER PLATZ INTO LEIPZIGER STRASSE, BERLIN, 1900. IN THE GROWING METROPOLIS, COMMON BOUNDARIES OF SPACE AND LOGISTICS WERE BLURRED TO CREATE WHAT AUGUST ENDELL, IN HIS ESSAY "THE BEAUTIFUL METROPOLIS" (1908), DESCRIBED AS A NEW WORLD OF "FANTASTIC FORMS."

For Rathenau and Twain, utilizing Chicago produced not only a different understanding of Berlin but a different kind of city altogether. Here, a complex amalgam of urban conditions from both sides of the Atlantic created a compounded modern metropolis–a "German Chicago–that existed at the intersection of the most radical aspects and trends of modern urbanization. Both authors hinted at the construction of an alternative metropolis that was no longer driven by history, culture, or form but by the acceleration of metropolitan forces (ultimately turning up the volume on aspects commonly considered as challenges to urban and architectural culture). The conflation of the two cities sped up what many considered as their problems and by doing so launched them into the present–describing an "apocalyptic urbanism," where the city's downfall would not only become its salvation but the acceleration of these "harmful" conditions was now seen as the prerequisite for a truly modern environment. But this kind of hyper-urbanism had yet to be fully understood.

BERLIN'S CHICAGO

In 1904, a group of German intellectuals traveled to the US as delegates of the Congress of Arts and Science that was organized in conjunction with the World Exhibition in St. Louis. Among them were the sociologists Werner Sombart, Ferdinand Tönnies, and Max Weber, who were deeply invested in questions concerning the modern city and

MAP OF CHICAGO SHOWING THE SPREAD OF THE GREAT FIRE IN RED, 1871. ILLUSTRATING THE EXTENSIVE DAMAGE CAUSED BY THE FIRE, AN APPARENT FAILURE OF THE CITY, THE MAP SIMULTANEOUSLY SUGGESTS THE NEW GROUND FOR URBAN DEVELOPMENT AND EXPANSION THAT THE FIRE LAID BARE. REVERSING THE DISASTER INTO A PROJECTIVE READING OF THE FUTURE, THE *CHICAGO TRIBUNE* ANNOUNCED IN MARCH 1873: "CHICAGO WAS SET FORWARD TEN YEARS BY THE FIRE."

saw their transatlantic voyage as an opportunity to visit "das Großstadtland"– the land of the metropolis, as Sombart described the US. Chicago left a particularly strong impression on these figures as the purest representation of modern urbanization. For Weber, it was a "monstrous city which even more than New York was the crystal-lization of the American spirit." Confronting the city for the first time, he recalled that it felt as though they were being "shaken out of a state of reverie and somnolence." Wandering through Chicago, they observed: "Look, this is what modern reality is like."[14] The lack of precedent for the city was what made them tremor.

Rhetorically asking: "What have Nuremberg and Chicago in common?" Sombart was quick to reply: "Nothing!"[15] As the most rational outcome of modern urban development, the American metropolis could not be reconciled with older, more established cities. To emphasize this divide, Chicago was defined as the prototypical American city and ur-metropolis. The former, Sombart associated with the grid that made expansion possible and was the rationalized infrastructure for urban export, while the latter was achieved through the city's "lack of history," as he called it. Chicago, rebuilt in record time after the 1871 fire according to modern standards and far beyond its earlier image, was seen as a new city with a negligible urban past that made the future seem attractive and tangible.

For Tönnies, the city's lack of history played an even more central role: "The American nation differentiates itself from older, more naturally and gradually grown nations through its removal from tradition and its lack of history."[16] This in turn, he argued, created an environment that devoted itself to technological advances while simultaneously hindering a common aesthetic understanding. Sombart and Tönnies problematized the often-cited lack of tradition and history as an inadequate condition while simultaneously hinting at what Johann Wolfgang von Goethe had long before described as the potential of the present that one could find in the US.[17] Local architects within Chicago, however, best summarized the lack of history that German visitors sought to grasp but so far were unable to comprehend fully. John Wellborn Root, of Burnham & Root, spoke during a lecture of an "America [that is] free of artistic tradition":

Our freedom begets license, it's true. We do shocking things, we produce works of architecture [...] irredeemably bad; we try crude experiments that result in disaster. Yet somehow in this mass of ungoverned energies lies the principle of life.[18]

For Root, the lack of history was associated with a degree of freedom that encouraged the surpassing of established norms and conventions. As such, Chicago became the perfect testing ground for crude architectural experiments. It became a model city that feared no past and, therefore, no failure. Numerous examples give evidence for Root's claim: the raising of the city's notoriously flat terrain to achieve better drainage (beginning in the early 1850s) and the reversal of the Chicago River that made Lake Michigan its source to secure safe drinking water for the city (achieved in 1900) are two massive endeavors that were not only responses to catastrophe but began as a series of failed implementations. The turn-around of the river's current, for example, was first celebrated in 1871, when chief engineer Ellis Chesbrough succeeded in reversing the river only to realize several months later that the sizeable effort to dredge the river was negated as silt accumulated,

157

reversing the river once more to its original state. Indeed, most Europeans were first introduced to Chicago as the city that made its river "run uphill" and that lifted itself out of its mud as the German *Bauzeitung* reported in 1868. Possibly the most vibrant description of this urban climate comes from Chicago's own Louis Sullivan:

[The city] is young, clumsy, foolish, its architectural sins are unstable, captious and fleeting; it can pull itself down and rebuild itself in a generation [...] it has done and can do great things when the mood is on [...] One must indeed be incurably optimistic even momentarily to dream such a dream.[19]

By speaking of "optimism," Sullivan adds an important characteristic that for architects would make it possible to not only survive in an urban climate where architecture evolves under metropolitan pressures, but that is required for a new species of architects to excel beyond the two primary models: the visionary utopian dreamer versus the pragmatic problem-solver. After all, the architectural impulses, vividly declared ambitions, and short-lived monuments are a display of the optimism

158 VIEW OF THE RAISING OF THE BRIGGS HOUSE, CHICAGO, CA. 1866. DURING THE 1850S AND 1860S, CHICAGO RAISED THE GROUND PLANE OF ITS CENTRAL DISTRICT ABOVE THE MUD TO IMPROVE DRAINAGE AND MAKE ROOM FOR A SEWER SYSTEM. AT FIRST, BUILDINGS WERE LIFTED INDIVIDUALLY, BUT SOON ENTIRE BLOCKS WERE PLACED ONTO THOUSANDS OF JACKS AT A TIME.

of the city just as buoyancy is understood as a required trait for the architect. In Chicago, the utopian dreamer meets the problem-solver, promoting a kind of visionary pragmatism. For Sullivan and Root, Chicago was the laboratory for modernity and, even more important, a zone in which artistic and stylistic traditions were suspended. Therefore, Sullivan's note should also be understood as a call for architects to no longer rely on historical precedents but to use the conditions of the existing city as a springboard for architectural experimentation.

METROPOLITAN ARCHITECTURE

The sheer height of Chicago's Masonic Temple (Burnham & Root, 1892), the simplicity and monumentality of the Monadnock Building (Burnham & Root, 1891), and the programmatic diversity of the Auditorium Building (Adler & Sullivan, 1889) might be the clearest articulation of an architecture driven by the forces of the metropolis. These buildings constituted a new kind of architecture that was analogous to descriptions by Karl Scheffler, the Berlin architectural critic, who formulated in 1907 a theory of architecture that argued for modern buildings to emerge solely from within the culture of the metropolis and its trading systems, population surge, urban density, and consumerism. Whereas Viennese architect Otto Wagner had previously declared modern life to be the sole departure point for a new architecture, Scheffler intimately linked the urbanity of the metropolis to what later was theorized as modernity's creation of "normativity out of itself."[20] The modern city had brought about spatial organizations, programmatic tensions, and material conditions that Scheffler understood as emergent archi-

VIEW OF THE ELEVATED TRAIN AT DENNEWITZ AND BÜLOW STREETS, BERLIN, 1905. CHICAGO'S SYSTEM OF ELEVATED TRAINS WAS EMBRACED AND ACCELERATED IN BERLIN TO CONCEIVE AN URBANISM OF THE INTERIOR, IN WHICH THE DYNAMICS OF THE METROPOLIS ENTERED INTO ARCHITECTURE.

tectural paradigms. These presented not only "unlimited possibilities" but, more specifically, the emergence of a new kind of architecture: *Großstadtarchitektur*, i.e. metropolitan architecture.[21]

Influenced by Tönnies's analysis of "Chicago without history," Scheffler spoke of Berlin as the most American of all European cities and, even more poignantly, as "the capital of all modern ugliness."[22] With the latter note he aimed at the city's willing embrace of a modern economy, industrial culture, and fast-paced urbanity.

Scheffler launched one of the most devastating critiques of Berlin's Americanization, while at the same time hinting at the unprecedented potential emerging from this new condition. "Nowhere," he argued, "is the character of modern building art-in positive and negative terms-more instructive [than in Berlin]."[23] This American city in Europe, with its lack of traditional backgrounds resembling its American counterpart, differed dramatically from more established cities like Munich or Dresden:

The young city of Berlin has none of the juxtaposing characteristics of old and new; instead there is a condition of indifference, which is surely regrettable in how the city appears from the outside, yet it also facilitates other aspects [...] Only the lax and faceless conditions of Berlin with its willingness to receive everything that is new-whether it be good or bad-allows Berlin to become paradigmatic [for modernity].[24]

Berlin became here part of the rhetorical comparison that Sombart had previously drawn, only this time Scheffler found a city that had everything in common with Chicago. What he saw in Berlin's condition of indifference is twofold: on the one

160   "GLEISDREIECK," RAILWAY INTERSECTION OF THE THREE MAJOR BRANCHES OF THE BERLIN SUBWAY, BERLIN, 1901. FOR SOME, GLEISDREIECK WAS THE ULTIMATE EXPRESSION OF METROPOLITAN FORMLESSNESS, WHILE FOR OTHERS, IT PRESENTED A SPACE OF OPPORTUNITIES IN WHICH NEW SPATIAL PARAMETERS COULD BE FOUND THAT WERE INDIGENOUS TO THE MODERN CITY.

hand, it created an undefined urban image that lacked the sophistication of older cities; on the other, it documented a categorical openness towards modern inventions. In other words, Berlin's carelessness about its appearance was the prerequisite for a total devotion towards everything modern. Deeply conflicted about the trajectory of the city, simultaneously mourning the loss of traditional urban form and celebrating the rational straightforwardness of the American grid, Scheffler addressed this dualism by noting: "[W]here unconditional affirmation is impossible and negation of the historically given is equally pathetic, one can only look towards its destiny [...] where one forgets words like beauty and ugliness."[25] Rather than unrestricted embrace or vehement resistance, Scheffler suggests that one must suspend preconceived aesthetic judgments in order to productively engage the formless metropolis, for it presented the only effective position within modernity.

In Scheffler's eyes, a modern architecture could only emerge from within the metropolis since architectural inventiveness occurred not in spite of the formless modern city, as illustrated by sites such as the infrastructural concoction of Gleisdreieck, but "especially because the urban formlessness created *Spielraum* [margin, room to play] for unlimited possibilities."[26] By taking reference from metropolises in the US, Scheffler began to see the potentials of Berlin's "un-designed" and matter-of-fact sites within the city. By not conforming to conventions of urban or architectural form, these locations would become the very vestige in which alternative points of view were able to develop and new architectural paradigms were to emerge.

161 LEFT: ALFRED MESSEL, WERTHEIM DEPARTMENT STORE AT LEIPZIGER STRASSE, BERLIN, 1908. WHILE BERLIN WAS LATE TO EMBRACE THE DEPARTMENT STORE, WERTHEIM BROUGHT A NEW SCALE, TRANSPARENCY, AND COMPLEXITY TO THE BUILDING TYPE THROUGH AN INSTRUMENTALIZATION OF TECHNOLOGY AND SPATIALIZATION OF COMMERCE.
RIGHT: BURNHAM & ROOT, MONADNOCK BUILDING, CHICAGO, 1891. DESIGNED AS THE LARGEST OFFICE BUILDING IN THE WORLD, THE MONADNOCK BECAME AN ORGANIZATIONAL CONSTRUCT THAT ABBREVIATES ARTISTIC GESTURES AND AMPLIFIES THE FORCES OF THE MODERN CITY.

In his book *Die Architektur der Großstadt* (Architecture of the Metropolis) from 1913, Scheffler contextualized this idea, aiming to show the architectural power of the modern city. He observed the uniformity, legibility, and typology of apartment buildings under construction and not yet adorned by ornamentation, the straight-forwardness of industrial warehouses that seemingly related only to the needs of production and infrastructural conditions, and the department store as a new building type giving expression to commodity culture. Warehouses, apartment buildings, and department stores were understood as products of metropolitan trading systems, population surges, urban density, and the spatialization of commodity culture–simultaneously approximating the formless city and the formative capacities of architecture.

The Wertheim Department Store (designed by Berlin architect Alfred Messel and built in phases between 1897 and 1906) was of particular importance for Scheffler, who believed that the Americanization of Berlin "forced [...] [Messel] to find a clear and monumental expression of the spirit of the new time."[27] Messel himself was less at ease with his design; as contemporaries recall, he was apparently startled at the sight of his invention and "was deeply shocked when he saw emerging the naked pillar system of the Wertheim façade."[28] Interestingly, in 1889 Root battled with similar emotions. When seeing a revised drawing of the Monadnock Building, he was "indignant at first over this project of a brick box" entirely stripped of any ornamentation.[29]

162

Both architects, so it seems, had unintentionally created a new building paradigm that they could no longer recognize and were at first frightened by their newest invention–a creation directly from the Frankensteinian laboratory, the metropolis. The projects that Root and Messel perceived as architectural "outcasts" and had to come to terms with, would set the following generation of metropolitan architects free as they began to recognize these buildings as a powerful blend of forces assembled from the modern city. In Chicago, it was viewed as a manifestation of "a direct singleness of purpose"[30] and Berlin's practitioners were ultimately "captivated by its clarity and dignity."[31]

CHICAGOISM

Critiqued for having a past but no history, a society but no community, and an industrial culture but no works of art, Chicago had first compromised Berlin through its
Americanization; ultimately, however, it pointed at what the city gained as a result of
this freedom from historical, communal, urban, and artistic constraints. Scheffler's
contribution to the discussion of the relationship between the two cities was a reworking of terminology, making the Americanization of Berlin an essential attribute for
bringing the city to a modern "conclusion," or better, to a state of constant becoming.
As such, the never-ceasing incompleteness of modernity was, for Scheffler, most clearly
expressed in the imminent and always pending urbanity of Berlin. The city that
"overnight" had become modern was seen as the incubator of this modernity that
"was condemned always to become and never to be."[32] The quintessential conditions
of modernity, previously defined as "transitory, fugitive, and contingent"[33] were
now linked to a formless urban maelstrom that was in a perpetual state of advance-

SEGMENT OF "PHANTOM CHICAGO," ORIGINALLY PRODUCED AS A ONE HUNDRED-FOOT-LONG DRAWING FOR THE 13TH INTERNATIONAL ARCHITECTURE BIENNALE IN VENICE, 2012.
TRANSCRIBING HISTORICAL AND ARCHITECTURAL DREAMS AND NIGHTMARES FROM ACROSS THE TWENTIETH CENTURY, THIS WORK OFFERS A VISION OF CHICAGO THAT IS NOT REAL
BUT VIVIDLY EXISTS IN OUR ARCHITECTURAL CONSCIOUSNESS. HERE, YESTERDAY'S AMBITIONS PRODUCE A PARALLEL CITY CAPABLE OF PRODUCTIVELY ENGAGING TOMORROW'S
FAILURES AS TEST-BEDS FOR IDEAS.

ment, always striving towards culmination without the possibility of ever reaching it.
        What Scheffler detected in Berlin and understood as the inescapable and
unending stipulation of urban modernity was for others an attitude that could as well
be undercut by the appeal for a more soothing urban condition under the auspices
of reconciliation with the past and comfort within the present. After all, Chicago today

bears little of the previous restlessness and desire to extrapolate modern conditions. Remarks from the late nineteenth century appear suddenly like prophesies as they foresaw the risk of the city eventually yielding to the charm of having its own history, of wanting to perfect its culture, and seeking its declarative urban and architectural forms. Predicting Chicago's future, a French architect in 1893 warned that it might eventually "succumb to the temptation to be refined."[34] To finalize the image of the city and complete a process that naturally avoids conclusion meant cancelling modernity and retiring into a state of comfort and stagnation.

While Chicago was at first Berlin's forecaster and hourglass that propelled the city to catch up to the present and realize its tendencies towards modernity, Berlin's earlier image of Chicago could be just as productive for Chicago's current state of affairs. Or, to use Marshall Berman's notion of a projective engagement with modernity: "To appropriate the modernities of yesterday can be at once a critique of the modernities of today and an act of faith in the modernities [...] of tomorrow and the day after tomorrow."[35] Berlin's fascination with Chicago, its comparative reading and extrapolation of urban qualities–including its failures–might here offer a catalytic reading where the Chicagoism that propelled Berlin is now thrown back onto the city of its origin. This new engagement with the city would be less about missed opportunities in the recent past than about openings in today's immediate future.

NOTES

This essay is partially based on my dissertation "The Formless Metropolis" (University of Pennsylvania, School of Design, 2008) and research conducted in preparation for an exhibition I curated at the Thirteenth International Architecture Biennale in Venice (2012), entitled "City Works." Thanks go to the School of Architecture at the University of Illinois at Chicago for the continued support of my research, the students at the school for their insightful discoveries during seminars on the topic, and my research team at the Visionary Cities Project. I am also grateful for the support I received in Berlin at the Akademie der Künste, the Landesarchiv, and the Stadtmuseum as well as in Chicago at the Art Institute and the History Museum. In addition, I would like to thank Jonathan Mekinda (co-editor of this volume) for his editorial input.

[1] Elias Colbert and Everett Chamberlin, *Chicago and the Great Conflagration* (Cincinnati and New York: C. F. Vent, 1872), p. 19; and, Martin Andersen Nexo, "Deutschlandbriefe," in *Reiseschilderungen (Reden und Artikel)*, vol. 1 (Berlin: Dietz, 1956). All translations are by the author, unless noted otherwise.

[2] Baedeker, *Berlin and Its Environs, Handbook for Travelers* (Leipzig: K. Baedeker, 1908), p. v.

[3] Charles Werner Haxthausen and Heidrun Suhr, eds., *Berlin: Culture and Metropolis* (Minneapolis: University of Minnesota Press, 1991), pp. 37-38.

[4] Alfred Lichtwark, 1894. Here quoted from Benjamin Carter Hett, *Death in the Tiergarten: Murder and Criminal Justice in the Kaiser's Berlin* (Cambridge, MA: Harvard University Press, 2004), p. 12.

[5] Reinhard Baumeister, *Stadterweiterungen in technischer, baupolizeilicher und wirtschaftlicher Beziehung* (Berlin: Ernst & Korn, 1876), p. 12.

[6] Julius Langbehn, *Rembrandt als Erzieher. Von einem Deutschen* (Weimar: Alexander Duncker Verlag, 1922), first published in 1890.

[7] Sara Jane Lippincott, uses "lightning city" to describe Chicago in *New Life in New Lands: Notes of Travel* (New York: J. B. Ford and Company, 1873) and David Macrae, in his book *The Americans at Home*, vol. 2 (Edinburgh: Edmonston and Douglas, 1970), titled his chapter on Chicago "The Lightning City."

[8] For one of the best studies of Chicago's development as prototypical American city and the perception of this city by foreign visitors, see Arnold Lewis, *An Early Encounter with Tomorrow* (Chicago: University of Illinois Press, 1997).

[9] For further reading on the German perception of the US, see Ulrich Ott, *Amerika ist anders: Studien zum Amerikabild in deutschen Reiseberichten des 20. Jahrhunderts* (Frankfurt: Lang, 1991).

[10] William Thomas Stead, *The Americanization of the World: The Trend of the Twentieth Century* (London: Horace Markley Publishing, 1901). For further reading on the understanding of US influence on Germany, see Frank Trommler, "The Rise and Fall of Americanism in Germany," in Frank Trommler and Joseph McVeigh, eds., *America and the Germans: An Assessment of a Three-hundred-Year History* (Philadelphia: University of Pennsylvania Press, 1985); Alf Lüdtke, Inge Marßolek, and Adelheid von Saldern, eds., *Amerikanisierung. Traum und Alptraum im Deutschland des 20. Jahrhunderts* (Stuttgart: Franz Steiner Verlag, 1996); Alexander Schmidt, *Reise in die Moderne* (Berlin: Akademie-Verlag, 1997).

[11] Walter Rathenau, *Die Schönste Stadt der Welt* (Berlin: Philo, 2001), p. 23. First published in *Die Zukunft*, 26 (1899).

[12] Ibid., p. 23: "Spreeathen ist tot und Spreechicago wächst heran."

[13] Mark Twain, "The German Chicago," in *The Complete Essays of Mark Twain* (Garden City, NY: Doubleday & Company, 1963), pp. 87–89.

[14] Marianne Weber, *Max Weber: A Biography*, trans. Harry Zohn (New York: John Wiley & Son, 1975), p. 285, 287. For further reading on Weber's impressions of America, see Lawrence A. Scaff, *Max Weber in America* (Princeton: Princeton University Press, 2011). For a thorough study of Berlin's relationship to Chicago in the urban literature around 1900, see Ralf Thiers and Dietmar Jazbinsek, "Embleme der Moderne. Berlin und Chicago in Stadttexten der Jahrhundertwende," in *Schriftenreihe der Forschungsgruppe "Metropolenforschung"* (Berlin: Wissenschaftszentrum Berlin, 1999).

[15] Werner Sombart, *Warum gibt es in den Vereinigten Staaten keinen Sozialismus?* (Tübingen: J. C. B. Mohr, 1906), p. 14.

[16] Ferdinand Tönnies, "Die nordamerikanische Nation," *Deutschland. Monatsschrift für die gesamte Kultur*, 4–5 (1906), p. 577.

[17] Johann Wolfgang von Goethe "Den Vereinigten Staaten," in *Nachgelassene Werke*, vol. 16 (Stuttgart: Cotta, 1842): *"Amerika, du hast es besser // Als unser Kontinent, der alte, // Hast keine verfallene Schlösser // Und keine Basalte. // Dich stört nicht im Innern, // Zu lebendiger Zeit, // Unnützes Erinnern // Und vergeblicher Streit. // Benutzt die Gegenwart mit Glück! // Und wenn nun eure Kinder dichten, // Bewahre sie ein gut Geschick // Vor Ritter-, Räuber- und Gespenstergeschichten."*

[18] John Wellborn Root, c. 1890. Here quoted from Lewis Mumford, *The Brown Decades: A Study of the Arts in America*, 1865–1895 (New York: Dover Publications, 1971), p. 60.

[19] Louis H. Sullivan, *Kindergarten Chats* (New York: Dover Publications, 1980), p. 111. First published in *Interstate Architect & Builder*, 1901–02.

[20] Jürgen Habermas, *The Philosophical Discourse of Modernity: Twelve Lectures*, trans. Frederick Lawrence (Cambridge, MA: MIT Press, 1990), p. 7.

[21] Ibid., p. 19, and Karl Scheffler, *Die Architektur der Großstadt* (Berlin: Bruno Cassirer Verlag, 1913). It is also important to remember that later modernists such as Ludwig Hilberseimer defined metropolitan

architecture as driven by the "economy of the moment and its matter-of-factness, material conditions, and construction techniques" (Ludwig Hilberseimer, *Großstadtarchitektur* [Stuttgart: Julius Hoffmann, 1927], p. 98.), whereas in the discourse around 1910, metropolitan architecture was more intimately linked with the modern city. More than half a century after Scheffler's publication, the term reappeared in its earlier characteristics in the founding of the Office for Metropolitan Architecture (1975) and the publication of *Delirious New York* (1978).

[22] Karl Scheffler, *Berlin–Ein Stadtschicksal* (Berlin: E. Reiss, 1910), p. 200. Berlin, Scheffler argued, had developed like an American city in which capitalist economy became an all-regulating force, creating a city of formless materialist urbanity. As the title of the book – *Berlin - Destiny of the City* – suggests, the development of the city was at stake. Looking towards the American metropolis promised to help to better understand what the future might hold for Berlin.

[23] Karl Scheffler, *Moderne Baukunst* (Berlin: Julius Bard, 1907), p. 1.

[24] Ibid., p. 1.

[25] Ibid., p. 12.

[26] Scheffler, *Berlin–Ein Stadtschicksal*, pp. 18-19.

[27] Ibid., p. 197.

[28] Walter Curt Behrendt, *Alfred Messel: Mit einer einleitenden Betrachtung von Karl Scheffler* (Berlin: Bruno Cassirer Verlag, 1911), pp. 28-29.

[29] Harriet Monroe, *John Wellborn Root: A Study of His Life and Work* (Cambridge, MA: The Riverside Press, 1896), p. 141.

[30] Louis H. Sullivan, *The Autobiography of an Idea* (New York: Dover Publications, 1956), p. 309.

[31] Bruno Taut, cited in Iain Boyd Whyte, *Bruno Taut and the Architecture of Activism* (Cambridge, UK: Cambridge University Press, 1982), p. 17. Peter Behrens praised Messel already in 1909 for his ability to fuse styles within a modern framework in his article "Alfred Messel: Ein Nachruf," *Frankfurter Zeitung* (Morgenblatt) (April 6, 1909), p. 225.

[32] Scheffler, *Berlin–Ein Stadtschicksal*, p. 219.

[33] Charles Baudelaire, "The Painter of Modern Life" in *The Painter of Modern Life and Other Essays*, trans. Jonathan Mayne (London: Phaidon Press, 1965), p. 13.

[34] Jaques Hermant, "L'art à l'exposition de Chicago," *Gazette des beaux-arts*, 73 (September 1893), p. 242.

[35] Marshall Berman, *All That Is Solid Melts into Air: The Experience of Modernity* (New York: Simon and Schuster, 1982), p. 36.

WATERWORLD

JOHN MCMORROUGH

168

If, previously, architecture arose from plenitude, as a surplus of money, labor, effort, etc., in the future the economies of scarcity will increasingly drive architectural ambition. As in the movie *Waterworld*, where even with a ubiquity of water, fresh water was in short supply, UrbanLab's Free Water District posits a future scenario in which the Great Lakes become the new OPEC, as fresh water supplants oil as the scarcest of commodities. In this peak-water condition, the economic activity of this aquatic free-trade zone has the collateral effect of architectural freedom.

The district is a multi-functional planning proposal that incorporates education, recreation, and industry. It is composed of two systems: one of building, the other of landscape, each a singular multiplicity. For the buildings, a monolithic extrusion jumps over and around itself, snaking around the site, becoming along its length a variety of morphing typologies: walls become bar buildings which then form courtyards, then perimeter blocks, creating a city unto itself. The landscape is a grid of circles, on first inspection, all the same, similar to crop irrigation or a printer dot screen. These circles plan a series of spaces: circular plazas or bulbous domes, both of which conceal a variety of activities underneath.

In the Free Water District we see the extension of rational singularities (lines and circles) into manifest multiplicities. Although *Waterworld*'s Mariner (Kevin Costner) lamented that "nothing's free in Waterworld," the District is a vision of possibility, enhanced, rather than limited, by its proximity to the possible. If the metropolis was the concretization of capital's accumulation, then the Free Water District represents the fluidity of an intelligent resource management.

GENERATIVE ATMOSPHERE

Atmosphere is a notion that only sporadically receives the attention it deserves from the architectural milieu. And yet atmosphere, or the ability to capture and produce it, is an essential quality when it comes to the perception and conception of architectural space. Cultural critic Siegfried Kracauer wrote in *The Mass Ornament* how the most significant revelations about the nature of the modern metropolis is in the surfaces, ephemera, and margins of everyday life. He also hinted at how spatial atmosphere arises from transient aspects of use and popular practice, as much as from physical environments. Decades later, Peter Zumthor would be one of the rare architectural voices that again addressed the significance of atmosphere in architecture. He would refer to "things themselves, the people, the air, noises, sound, colors, material presences, textures, and forms too" as the atmospheric elements that make a space memorable. In this context, however, Zumthor offered architecture as only a finely tuned backdrop, a physical receptacle in which atmosphere could flourish. What if atmosphere itself, fleeting and fluid as it may be, became the driver for generating space? This is the question that some recent architectural practitioners have dealt with. Sean Lally and his office Weathers have explored (similar to François Roche or Philippe Rahm) atmospheric conditions as an experimental basis from which to breed spatial form. "Environmental Typologies," as Lally calls his most recent experiments, are proposed to populate plazas and parks in Chicago's neighborhoods. Here, he investigates the opportunities associated with materials and energies "believed to be beyond our reach of control on the exterior." To address how the insubstantial may originate environments that respond once more to human emotion – in a world in which digital tools continuously instigate new materialities – this may indeed be a fascinating path to recapture atmosphere again for architecture.

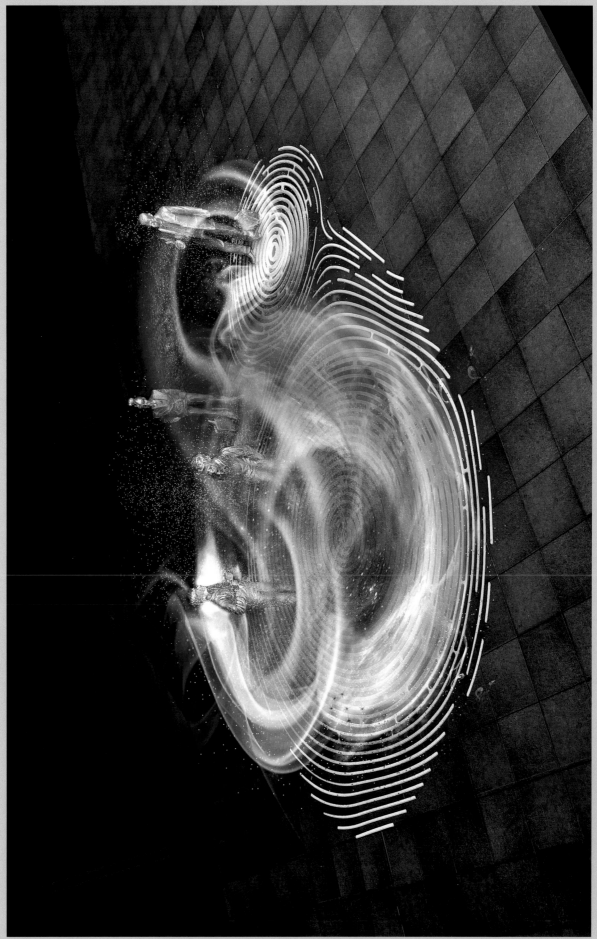

ACKNOWLEDGMENTS

This project began as a panel at the annual meeting of the Society of Architectural Historians in 2010, which convened in Chicago that year. We, therefore, want to thank the SAH, Dianne Harris, chair of that meeting, and, most of all, the speakers who participated in that initial effort: Penelope Dean, John Harwood, Igor Marjanović, and Joanna Merwood-Salisbury. *Chicagoisms*, or "Chicago in the World" as the project was called then, would not have taken shape without that first productive gathering and the discussions that followed in its wake. We are also grateful for the constructive dialogue and encouragement that we received from many of our colleagues when we began to consider the possibility of a publication on this topic. In particular, we want to acknowledge Robert Bruegmann, Marcia Lausen, Zoë Ryan, Robert Somol, and David van Zanten, who all helped the project in their varying capacities at critical moments in its development.

This volume would not have been possible without the generous financial support of the Graham Foundation for Advanced Studies in the Fine Arts, and we thank Sarah Herda, Director of the Foundation, for that crucial endorsement. In the later stages of our work, we received additional support from the College of Architecture, Design, and the Arts and the Office of the Vice Chancellor for Research at the University of Illinois at Chicago; our thanks to Dean Judith Kirshner and Interim Dean Robert Somol, as well as Vince Paglione, Special Assistant to the Dean, and Luis Vargas, Executive Director of the Office of Research Services. We would also like to recognize Lauren van Damme, Assistant Director of the School of Architecture, who handled the complicated logistics of the project so tirelessly.

Several archives and collections have been central to this project and we would like to thank Alison Fisher in the Department of Architecture and Design at the Art Institute of Chicago, Melanie Emerson and the staff at the Ryerson & Burnham Libraries at the Art Institute of Chicago, Jessica Herczeg-Konecny and the research staff at the Chicago History Museum, John Ferry at the Estate of R. Buckminster Fuller, and Valerie Harris in the Special Collections Department of the University of Illinois at Chicago. A number of other individuals were instrumental to the production of this volume. The photographers Steve Hall, Michelle Litvin, and Philippe Ruault generously shared their work. As graphic designer, Jörg Becker has been a rewarding collaborator and interlocutor who fundamentally shaped the way the book looks today. Working with Park Books has also been tremendously rewarding, as their attention to detail and commitment to the book as an object and artifact have been central to the final form of this publication. We must also acknowledge our editor, Ria Stein. Ria has been a champion of this project from an early stage and we are profoundly grateful for her persistent support.

172

As with any collection of essays, this book would not exist without the various "voices" who have convened in its pages. Our deepest appreciation goes, therefore, to the many authors who engaged our mutual topic by undertaking new research, challenging established histories and perceptions, and formulating new arguments and assessments. We are indebted to all of them not only for their insightful contributions, but also for their enthusiasm, generosity, and patience.

Alexander Eisenschmidt
Jonathan Mekinda

CONTRIBUTORS

WILLIAM F. BAKER is the Partner in Charge of Structural Engineering for Skidmore, Owings & Merrill LLP. He has led the structural design teams for numerous tall buildings, including the Burj Khalifa in Dubai, the world's tallest tower. In addition to tall buildings, Baker and his team have designed structures ranging in scale from small houses to major convention/exhibition centers. He is a frequent lecturer and is active in several professional organizations and societies.

BARRY BERGDOLL is the Meyer Schapiro Professor of Art History at Columbia University and curator at the Department of Architecture and Design at the Museum of Modern Art, New York. He is author and editor of numerous publications including *Karl Friedrich Schinkel: An Architecture for Prussia* (1994), *Mies in Berlin* (2001), and *Bauhaus 1919–1933: Workshops for Modernity* (2009). Bergdoll served as President of the Society of Architectural Historians from 2006 to 2008.

AARON BETSKY is the Director of the Cincinnati Art Museum. Active as a critic, writer, and lecturer on art, architecture, and design, he was the Director of the 11th Venice International Architecture Biennale. He is the author of over a dozen books, and his collected essays, *At Home in Sprawl,* were published in 2012 by RMIT Publishing.

ROBERT BRUEGMANN is a historian and critic of the built environment and Distinguished Professor Emeritus of Art History, Architecture, and Urban Planning at the University of Illinois at Chicago. He is the author of numerous articles and books, among them *The Architects and the City: Holabird & Roche of Chicago 1880–1918* (1998), *Sprawl: A Compact History* (2005), and *The Architecture of Harry Weese* (2010). His main areas of research are in architectural and urban history, landscape design, and historic preservation.

PENELOPE DEAN is Associate Professor of Architecture at the University of Illinois at Chicago. Her writings have appeared in *Architectural Design, Harvard Design Magazine, hunch, Log, Praxis,* and *TransScape.* Her research has been supported by grants from the Graham Foundation for Advanced Studies in the Fine Arts and a Visiting Scholars Residency at the Canadian Centre for Architecture at Montreal. She is founding editor of the architectural magazine *Flat Out.*

ALEXANDER EISENSCHMIDT is a designer, theorist, and Assistant Professor of Architecture at the University of Illinois at Chicago. His work investigates the productive tension between the modern city and architectural form – a topic on which he has published and lectured extensively. Eisenschmidt is the editor of *City Catalyst* (AD, 2012), curator of *City Works* for the 13th International Architecture Biennale in Venice, and founding partner of Studio Offshore.

PEDRO GADANHO is the Curator of Contemporary Architecture in the Department of Architecture and Design at the Museum of Modern Art, New York. Previously, he divided his activity between architecture, teaching, writing, and curating. He was the editor of *BEYOND* bookazine, writes the Shrapnel Contemporary blog, and is the author of *Arquitectura em Público*, which won the FAD Prize for Thought and Criticism in 2012.

ELLEN D. GRIMES is an Associate Professor at the School of the Art Institute of Chicago, where she teaches architectural design, technology, and theory. Previously she taught at the University of Illinois at Chicago and the Illinois Institute of Technology, and served as the executive editor of the *Journal of Architectural Education.*

DAVID H. HANEY is a Senior Lecturer in Architecture at the University of Kent (UK), Centre for Research in European Architecture. His work focuses on the relationship between landscape and architecture in the context of twentieth-century modernism. Haney's book *When Modern Was Green: Life and Work of Landscape Architect Leberecht Migge* was awarded SAH Elisabeth Blair MacDougall Book Award in 2013, and he recently translated Migge's *Garden Culture of the Twentieth Century* (1913) into English.

JOHN HARWOOD is Associate Professor for Modern and Contemporary Architectural History in the Department of Art at Oberlin College. He is an editor of *Grey Room*, a member of the architectural history collaborative Aggregate, and author of *The Interface: IBM and the Transformation of Corporate Design, 1945–1976* (University of Minnesota Press, 2011).

SANDY ISENSTADT teaches the history of modern architecture at the University of Delaware. His writings range over topics as varied as post-war reformulations of modern architecture, visual perception in the built environment, landscape views, and American material culture. He is currently working on a book examining novel luminous spaces introduced by electric lighting in the twentieth century.

SAM JACOB is a director of FAT Architecture, where he has been responsible for award-winning projects for clients including Selfridges and the BBC. His work has been exhibited at major institutions such as the Venice Biennale, MAK in Vienna, and the V&A in London. He is design critic for *Art Review*, contributing editor for *Icon*, and columnist for *Dezeen*. Jacob is currently a Clinical Professor of Architecture at the University of Illinois at Chicago and Director of the forthcoming Night School at the AA. He writes and edits *Strangeharvest.com.*

SYLVIA LAVIN is the author of *Kissing Architecture* (2011), *The Flash in the Pan and Other Forms of Architectural Contemporaneity* (2013), and the curator/editor of *Everything Loose Will Land*, an exhibition and catalog on art and architecture in the 1970s in LA (2013). Lavin is Director of the Ph.D. program in the Department of Architecture at UCLA, where she was Chairperson from 1996 to 2006.

MARK LEE is the Principal of Johnston Marklee & Associates. The Los Angeles-based firm has been engaged in a range of commissions in the US, Switzerland, Italy, Spain, Portugal, Chile, Argentina, and China since 1998. Mark Lee has taught at the ETH in Zurich, the Technical University of Berlin, Rice University, and UCLA, where he has served as Vice Chair.

ANDRES LEPIK is Professor for Architecture History and Curatorial Practice and Director of the Architecture Museum at the Technical University of Munich. He was curator at the Neue Nationalgalerie in Berlin and the Architecture and Design Department at the Museum of Modern Art in New York. In Berlin, he has presented exhibitions such as *Content: Rem Koolhaas and AMO/OMA"* (2003), and at MoMA he curated *Small Scale, Big Change: New Architectures of Social Engagement* (2010).

DAVID J. LEWIS is a founding Principal at LTL Architects in New York and an Associate Professor at Parsons The New School for Design. LTL is an award-winning practice; recipient of the National Design Award from the Cooper-Hewitt in 2007, exhibiting at the 2004 Venice Architecture Biennale, and, most recently, publishing their third monograph *Intensities* with Princeton Architectural Press.

MARK LINDER is Associate Professor in Architecture and Chancellor's Fellow in the Humanities at Syracuse University. He is the author of *Nothing Less than Literal: Architecture after Minimalism* (MIT Press, 2004) and is currently working on a book titled *Three Easy Mieses: That's Brutal, What's Modern?* on the alternative mid-century modernisms of Alison and Peter Smithson, Walter Segal, and John Hejduk.

BART LOOTSMA is a historian, critic, and curator in the fields of architecture, design, and the visual arts. He is a Professor for Architectural Theory and Head of the Institute for Architectural Theory, History, and Heritage Preservation at the University of Innsbruck.

WINY MAAS is one of the co-founding directors of the globally operating architecture and urban planning firm MVRDV, based in Rotterdam and Shanghai. He is Professor and Director of The Why Factory, a research institute for the future city, which he founded in 2008 at Delft University of Technology.

IGOR MARJANOVIĆ teaches architectural design and history at Washington University in St. Louis. Together with Katerina Rüedi Ray, he is a Principal of ReadyMade Studio and co-author of *Marina City: Bertrand Goldberg's Urban Vision*. His research focuses on pedagogy as a generator of wider architectural discourses, with an emphasis on the work of Alvin Boyarsky. His writings have appeared in *Critical Architecture, Chicago Architecture, AA Files, ARQ,* and other venues.

JOHN MCMORROUGH is a principal architect in the firm studioAPT and an Associate Professor at the University of Michigan Taubman College of Architecture and Urban Planning. As an architect McMorrough has worked for design offices in Kansas City, New York, Boston, and Rotterdam, and he has taught theory and design at the Yale School of Architecture, Massachusetts Institute of Technology, the Ohio State University, and the Institute of Architecture at the University of Applied Arts in Vienna.

JONATHAN MEKINDA is an Assistant Professor at the University of Illinois at Chicago with a joint appointment in the School of Design and the Department of Art History. He has written for journals such as *Design Issues* and the *Journal of Design History* and is currently working on a book entitled *Building the House of Man: Design and the Modern Home in Milan, 1930–1960*.

JOANNA MERWOOD-SALISBURY is Associate Professor of Architectural History at Parsons The New School for Design. She is the author of *Chicago 1890: The Skyscraper and the Modern City* (University of Chicago Press, 2009) and a co-editor of *After Taste: Expanded Practice in Interior Design* (Princeton Architectural Press, 2011). Her primary research area is the Chicago School of Architecture.

ALBERT POPE is an architect living in Houston, Texas. He is the Gus Sessions Wortham Professor of Architecture at Rice University and the author of numerous writings on contemporary urbanism, including the book *Ladders*.

BRETT STEELE is the Director of the Architectural Association (AA) School of Architecture in London and he directs AA Publications (Ltd.) as well as the school's Public Program. Articles, interviews, and essays by Steele have been published in many languages and he is a frequent lecturer, critic, and advisor at schools and organizations internationally.

STANLEY TIGERMAN is a principal at Tigerman McCurry Architects and a Fellow of the American Institute of Architects. He has designed buildings and installations throughout the world, from the US to Asia and across Europe, and his firm is the recipient of 169 design awards. Tigerman was selected to represent the United States at the 1976, 1980, and 2012 Venice Biennales. He is the former Director of the School of Architecture at the University of Illinois at Chicago and co-founded of ARCHEWORKS, which he directed for fourteen years.

KAZYS VARNELIS is Director of the Network Architecture Lab at Columbia University and co-founder of the conceptual architecture group AUDC, which published *Blue Monday* and has exhibited widely. He edited *The Infrastructural City, Networked Publics*, and *The Philip Johnson Tapes,* worked with the Center for Land Use Interpretation, and produced the *New City Reader* with Joseph Grima for the *Last Newspaper* exhibit at the New Museum in New York. His present book project is *The Network Turn: Culture After the Postmodern.*

SARAH WHITING has been Dean of the School of Architecture at Rice University since 2010. Additionally, she is a partner, along with Ron Witte, of WW, an architecture practice based in Houston. Her research and writing focus on how architecture can foster a public audience or what could also be called a collective subject.

MIRKO ZARDINI is an architect and, since 2005, the Director and Chief Curator of the Canadian Centre for Architecture. His research engages the transformation of contemporary architecture by questioning the assumptions on which architects operate today. Zardini has been editor for *Casabella* and *Lotus International* magazine and his writings have been widely published. He has taught at architecture schools in Europe and the United States, including Harvard University GSD, Princeton University SoA, Swiss Federal Polytechnic University (ETH) at Zurich, and the Federal Polytechnic at Lausanne (EPFL).

ILLUSTRATION CREDITS

Every effort has been made to trace the copyright ownership of the illustrations used in this volume, and we will correct any errors or omissions in subsequent editions. We are grateful to the many organizations and individuals who have given permission to reproduce photographs, drawings, and documents.

Cover: Photograph of Chicago by Alex Zyuzikov.

9: Library of Congress, Prints & Photographs Division, HABS, HABS ILL, 16-CHIG, 39-(Sheet 44 of 53).

11: Brooklyn Museum Archives. Visual materials [6.1.016]: World's Columbian Exposition lantern slides. Ferris Wheel, Chicago, United States, 1893.

19: Courtesy of the Chicago History Museum.

21: Daniel H. Burnham and Edward H. Bennett, Plate 122 from the *Plan of Chicago*, 1909: Railway Station Scheme West of the River Between Canal and Clinton Streets, Showing the Relation with the Civic Center, 1905, Graphite and watercolor on paper, 88.7 x 200cm, On permanent loan to The Art Institute of Chicago from the City of Chicago, 22.148.1966, The Art Institute of Chicago.

24, 27: Laurence Booth, Stuart E. Cohen, Stanley Tigerman, and Benjamin Weese, *Chicago Architects*, 1976.

25: Oswald W. Grube, Peter C. Pran and Franz Schulze; David Norris, trans., *100 Years of Architecture in Chicago: Continuity of Structure and Form*, 1976.

26: Stanley Tigerman, *The Titanic*, 1978, Photomontage on paper, Approx. 28 x 35.7cm, Gift of Stanley Tigerman, 1984.802, The Art Institute of Chicago.

28-29: Oswald W. Grube, Peter C. Pran and Franz Schulze; David Norris, trans. and additional text *100 Years of Architecture in Chicago: Continuity of Structure and Form*, 1977.

30: Los Angeles Times Photographic Archive, Department of Special Collections, Charles E. Young Research Library, UCLA.

31: © Museum of Contemporary Art Chicago.

39: Frank Lloyd Wright, *Ausgeführte Bauten und Entwürfe von Frank Lloyd Wright*, 1910. Image courtesy of the Ryerson and Burnham Libraries, The Art Institute of Chicago.

41: © 2013 Artists Rights Society (ARS), New York / VBK, Vienna. Image courtesy of the Ryerson and Burnham Libraries, The Art Institute of Chicago.

43, 46-47, 51, 52, 53: Courtesy of Alvin Boyarsky Archive, London.

48, 49, 50: Courtesy of Wiley/*Architectural Design*.

59: Courtesy of the Estate of R. Buckminster Fuller.

61: Reproduction of negative HB-13809-L4, courtesy of the Chicago History Museum.

64, 66 (right), 70–71: Konrad Wachsmann, *The Turning Point of Building: Structure and Design*, 1961.

66 (left): *Arbeitsgemeinschaft für Forschung des Landes Nordrhein-Westfalen,* v. 136, 1967.

67, 68: *Bauen und Wohnen* 14 (October 1960).

72 (left, right): *Arts + Architecture* 84 (May 1967).

77: Courtesy of the Chicago History Museum.

79: Photograph by Hedrich Blessing (HB-41780), courtesy of the Goldberg Family Archives.

81 (left): *Architects' Journal*, January 3, 1946.

81 (right), 90: Charles Jencks, *Modern Movements in Architecture*, 1973.

82 (left): Photograph courtesy of Mark Linder.

82 (right), 83: Reyner Banham, "The New Brutalism," *Architectural Review* 118 (December 1955).

85 (left, right): Photograph by Nigel Henderson, 1953. Henderson Estate.

87: Reyner Banham, "On Trial: Mies van der Rohe: Almost Nothing Is Too Much," *Architectural Review* (August 1962).

88, 89: Reyner Banham, *The Age of the Masters*, 1975.

92 (left): Drawing reproduced from Philip Johnson, *Mies van der Rohe*, 1946. Courtesy of the Museum
   of Modern Art New York.

92 (right): Alison and Peter Smithson, Tulip Chair and Egg Chair (for House of the Future), 1956.
   Smithson Family Collection, London.

96-7: SOM, © McShane-Fleming Studios.

99: Stanley Tigerman, *The Titanic*, 1978, Photomontage on paper, Approx. 28 x 35.7cm, Gift of Stanley
   Tigerman, 1984.802, The Art Institute of Chicago.

101: Wendell Cox, "The Evolving Urban Form: Chicago," *New Geography*, 07/18/2011.
   http://www.newgeography.com/content/002346-the-evolving-urban-form-chicago, accessed 12/26/12.

104: Mies van der Rohe and Hilberseimer with students at the Armour Institute at The Art Institute
   of Chicago, Chicago, IL, 1942. Thomas R. Burleigh Collection, Ryerson and Burnham Archives,
   The Art Institute of Chicago.

106-7, 109-10: Drawings by and courtesy of Albert Pope.

113: Courtesy Greg Lynn FORM

115: © Philippe Ruault. Courtesy of OMA

118 (left, right), 119 (left), 125: The Museum of Modern Art/Licensed by SCALA/Art Resource, NY.

119 (right), 120 (left, right), 121 (left): Library of Congress.

121 (right): The New York Public Library/Art Resource, NY.

131: © Michelle Litvin

133: Image by City of Chicago. All rights reserved.

136: Daniel H. Burnham and Edward H. Bennett, Plate 132 from the *Plan of Chicago*, 1909: View, Looking
   West, of the Proposed Civic Center Plaza and Buildings, Showing it as the Center of the System of Arteries
   of Circulation and of the Surrounding Country, 1908, Graphite and watercolor on paper, 75.4 x 105.5 cm,
   On permanent loan to The Art Institute of Chicago from the City of Chicago, 28.148.1966,
   The Art Institute of Chicago.

137, 141: Werner Hegemann, *Der neue Bebauungsplan für Chicago*, 1910. Images courtesy of the
   Special Collections Department, Richard J. Daley Library, University of Illinois at Chicago.

142 (left, right), 143: Werner Hegemann, *Ein Parkbuch*, 1911.

147: © UNStudio: Ben van Berkel and Caroline Bos. Courtesy UNStudio

149: Steve Hall © Hedrich Blessing

142, 154: Courtesy of the Chicago History Museum.

153: *Map of Chicago with Comparison to Berlin* (Leipzig: Meyer, 1900). Courtesy of Alexander Eisenschmidt.

155-56, 158-61: Documentation of buildings in Berlin and Chicago, 1871-1908, Public Domain.

162-63: © Alexander Eisenschmidt. Courtesy of Visionary Cities Project/Alexander Eisenschmidt.

169: © UrbanLab, Sarah Dunn and Martin Felsen. Courtesy UrbanLab

171: © WEATHERS/Sean Lally. Courtesy Sean Lally

INDEX